FRANKLYN

V.C. SEALES

Also by Jean M Dorsinville

HONOR THY FATHER,
an Awakening

FRANKLYN V.E. SEALES

Life of an Artist
by

Jean M. Dorsinville

iUniverse, Inc.
Bloomington

FRANKLYN V.E. SEALES
LIFE OF AN ARTIST

iUniverse books may be ordered through booksellers or by contacting:

iUniverse
1663 Liberty Drive
Bloomington, IN 47403
www.iuniverse.com
1-800-Authors (1-800-288-4677)

ISBN: 978-1-4620-3331-7 (pbk)
ISBN: 978-1-4620-3332-4 (ebk)

Printed in the United States of America

iUniverse rev. date: 06/30/2011

CONTENTS

This book is dedicated to Lessie, whose selfless dedication and noble devotion for their wellbeing carried them through their formative years and into adult life. They are all eternally grateful.

PREFACE

When we sit back and reflect on significant events, evoke memories of people in our past, assess important aspects of our current lives, and how one man could have played such a transformative role in the journey of so many through life, it is not surprising, in this moment of calm reflection, that we find ourselves inspired to memorialize his remarkable achievements born of a compelling yearning, an insatiable appetite, an incurable drive to live his dreams.

Such was a man named Franklyn Vincent Ellison Seales, the natural born son of Francis Seales, a merchant seaman and government employee of English, Scottish and African ancestry and Olive Seales, nee Allen, a homemaker of Portuguese and native Carib Indian stock. He was the youngest of that family of five: three girls and two boys, born on 15 July 1952 in the small village of Calliaqua, St Vincent and the Grenadines, a former English colony that gained independence in 1979 while remaining within the British Commonwealth, part of the Windward Islands, the northern islands of the Lesser Antilles chain of islands, which lies at the eastern border of the Caribbean Sea. It's a tropical paradise for scuba diving, yachting and many other water sports that attract tourists from the European community, Asia, Africa, and the Americas. This idyllic setting ennobled young Franklyn to develop his God-given innate talents leading him on a wondrous journey in fulfillment of his dreams. We celebrate that he was the first native of the island to graduate from the prestigious Juilliard School in New York City that led him to appear on the silver screen in Hollywood.

Olive Seales was in labor for more than twelve hours, far longer than for her previous four children. It was agonizing going through the motion of delivering that child. Very strong menstrual cramps were coming in waves that made her belch out piercing screams that could be heard by the neighbors. The night grew darker as she waited for nature to take its course. She remained awake, being comforted by the midwife and the nanny, Lessie, at bedside wiping the sweat dripping profusely from her forehead, helping her sip a lukewarm cup of tea, refraining her from screaming but recommending sort of a ritualistic moaning and grunting to relieve the pain. The other children could not or did not want to sleep either, more excited about the birth of an addition to the family. Her husband was at sea like he had been for many years away from the family in quest of a job that promised much more than could be earned on the island. As the cock crowed and the first rays of sunlight rose over the horizon to bathe the room, the contractions became more intense and evenly spaced, signaling that the end was near. A loud and prolonged scream hung in the air of the tiny room before it rushed out the open windows and onto the street, followed by a transitory sound of silence, then, the unmistakable scream of a baby's first breath that replaced the fluid in his lungs, announcing he had finally arrived. Olive Seales had given birth to her second baby boy on that summer morning of July 15, 1952. His face was draped with a thin filmy membrane, the remnants of the amniotic sac that foretold great things according to legend that had been passed on through generations. Writings on this phenomenon conclude, "A baby born with a veil is destined for great things." *In medieval times the appearance of a veil or "Caul" on a newborn baby was seen as a sign of good luck. It was considered an omen that the child was destined for greatness. Gathering the Caul onto paper was considered an important tradition of childbirth: the midwife would rub a sheet of paper across the baby's head and face, pressing the material of the Caul onto the paper. The Caul would then be presented to the mother, to be kept as an heirloom. Medieval women often sold their Cauls to sailors for large sums of money because a caul was then also regarded as a valuable talisman against drowning.*

"Midwives are more likely to allow babies to be born in the Caul. Some midwives believe allowing children to be born in the Caul has spiritual significance; others simply think nature should be allowed to unfold as necessary, especially as there may be some physiological benefit to being born this way," says Kat Montgomery, a registered midwife in British Columbia, Canada, believes that being born in the Caul is much more prevalent than most doctors know. In her career, she has seen at least one in twenty five babies born in the Caul. She notes, "The baby comes out looking for a moment as if it is wearing nylons over its head. And then the membranes spontaneously rupture, peeling down over the face. Parents seem to love the fact that their unique birth and special baby have been marked by this elevated significance."

Many other legends also persisted over time. One popular legend went that a Caul bearer would be able to see the future or have dreams that come to pass. Many famous people throughout history were born with a Caul, among them were the great musician and entertainer, Liberace. Queen Christina of Sweden. Black artist Frank Albert Jones. Poet, Painter, sculptor, inventor and craftsman, Kahlil Gibran. Poet and member of the House of Lords, Lord Byron. Actress Lillian Gish, Sigmund Freud, Napoleon Bonaparte, the list is endless.

This unusual and rare phenomenon seen by the other children in the early hours of July 15 was soon forgotten as the baby's piercing screams reverberated throughout the house and stopped when he suckled at his mother's breast for his first meal. The older children, the three girls, left for school not the least concerned they had not slept a wink. Left home with their mother was four-year old Lennox. The nurse midwife assigned to the area of town, after making sure her patient's condition was ameliorating, finally bade goodbye to all and left for home.

"OLIVE"!!! A loud voice bellowed in the early morning hours—The cavalry had arrived. As was the custom, the neighbors opened the front door and invited themselves in to keep her company, bringing hot food for the entire family and, in addition, fresh vegetables: avocadoes or 'zabocas,' plantains, bananas, veggies; the family nanny, the 'venerable' Lessie, would prepare for the kids when

they returned from school for lunch. During the entire day and for days after, little Franklyn was passed from the hands of one neighbor to the other, a ritual that has survived for generations on that tiny tropical island.

In retrospect, Franklyn's life was already predestined by a series of unimaginable, mysterious, unexplainable conditions and forces that escaped our limited imaginations, yet directed him on a path that few are chosen to tread. To acknowledge Franklyn's life paths is to recognize the existence of the all seeing, all loving, omnipotent God. As his brother professes, *"Franklyn was born with a third eye: one who appears to know why he is here in this physical life. He comes equipped: he knows the path. Most of us will stumble, get lucky or be forever lost. Franklyn, came with a knowingness that is beyond the consciousness of most. It is very uncommon and unless one has been exposed to these special people, one will never know what I am talking about."*

We begin with the belief that nothing in this Universe materializes by happenstance or in a vacuum. We, in effect, are invoking the "Power of Intention" when we speak of Franklyn and his life one that attracted the essential that he was. It is almost beyond comprehension that given where they were born and the circumstances surrounding their lives, he had an energy and a light that transcended circumstances: that which is unstoppable and without resources, beyond his quantitative experiences. Franklyn, we can say was moving with an energy that can only be understood in terms of the supernatural. It is a given that the energy and the light that surrounded him was the power of the all-knowing. One can recall his brother's attempts to talk to Franklyn about this said altruism back in the late 70's and early 80's. He was, either unknowingly or purposely, unable to grasp what was conveyed to him, but it became apparent to everyone, even then, that he would be in danger of the disconnect if he persisted on ignoring the warnings. Somehow he could not or would not. Franklyn always experienced a sense of the awareness of people and their intensions. He had developed a certain intuition enabling him to discern characteristics that escape most. It is after all, a sixth sense. It is not something to explain, but rather something to appreciate as we embrace its presence within us. It is obvious that Franklyn intuitively understood his calling to the arts. He was selected and drawn to the energies. In St. Vincent, he touched people with his inner drive and vision which correlate with the energy of irresistibility. He was inexorable in his quest to win people over by his inner vision and love.

Franklyn knew the loneliness of being a creative person. Not many of his peers who were his constant companions recognized this value that comes with the gift of creativeness. This is something that originates deep from within that summons a powerful energy to become manifest, especially when often times the ones closest did not fully comprehend the depth and the power of the gift he carried from the time he was a young boy. In time they gradually learned to discover his life of inner solitude and pain. They lived to see the outcome. It took them years, but they finally reconciled with Franklyn's inner world and forward vision.

PART ONE

THE GENESIS

Mother Olive comes to an abrupt stop, momentarily muted, holding her breath, her eyelids distended, uncovering her eyes fixated on her eight-month-old Franklyn reaching for the leg of the chair with his tiny hands and pulling himself up to stand and take his first steps on the rugless hardwood floor of the bedroom. She claps excitedly while her little baby's mouth opens to draw a smile. She picks him up, brings him to her chest and hugs little Franklyn tightly before gently putting him down to watch him move around the room on his tiny little feet with atypical balance. This is four months earlier than her previous four children, she muses. Sensing she was witnessing the improbable, the door flies open, crashing against the side of the house: *"Look Lessie, Franklyn is walking . . . come and see . . . come quick!"* Olive's voice bellows at the top of her lungs, carrying a sound that can be easily mistaken for someone in distress. Lessie, the nanny, is in the backyard busily carrying her daily chores of washing the clothes and hanging them to dry under the hot tropical sun moderated by the balmy breeze that sways the tall mango trees pointing toward the clear blue open sky, when the sound of Olive's voice echoes in her ears. She drops everything and hurriedly rushes to the house to witness with eyes wide open. *"Baby Franklyn walkin' ah can't believe me eyes . . . yuh alright baby child?"* she exclaims with a hint of trepidation in her voice she can barely control. Even Lessie, who had much experience raising other people children, was shaking her head in disbelief, praying Ms Olive's baby is not under the influence of some malevolent spirit. *"ah gonna pray fuh him Ms Olive . . ."* she mutters once . . . twice . . . three times, barely able to contain her excitement.

Franklyn's tiny first steps on that day would grow into giant strides on the long journey that awaited him.

By his first year, this joyful baby boy was bouncing to the amusement of Mom and Dad and his siblings, as well as the villagers of Calliaqua who took a special interest in his development. Lessie, by now, had set aside her concerns that this baby boy had 'bad spirit' in him but would always preface a conversation with the words, "Lawdy, da chil' is blessed . . . lawdy, lawdy . . ." Not only was he walking but he began to express words usually heard spoken by a three-year-old, further deepening her puzzlement.

Lessie was not only the nanny but more accurately the surrogate mother as well; the one who was present to attend to the needs of the five children of Olive and Francis Seales. A physically imposing, big boned, statuesque-five feet ten inches barefoot tall-Amazonian-like illiterate woman born of parents that occupied the lower societal strata on that island whose lack of a formal education confined her to a life of quasi servitude for families that hired her. She had a smooth evenly ebony-colored skin that glistened in the sunlight. Her hair was matted tightly on her scalp she wrapped in an ever present bandana that captured the beads of sweat dripping from her head.

Her arms were unusually strong, borne out of tilling the land of her parents: planting fruit trees, chopping wood, planting vegetables, lifting rocks, harvesting the land, climbing coconut trees, mango trees, avocado trees, breadfruit trees . . . customary practices for survival that required minimum cash outlay but kept many stomachs full. Her eyes reflected a sensitive soul that became manifest in the care she provided to the children. She was in her early twenties when she joined the Seales household: never married and oftentimes the butt of teasing from the children and others in the village who would affectionately taunt her,

"You have a boyfriend, Lessie?"
". . . Me don't need no boyfriend,"

she would answer with a sheepish grin she never outgrew that led to speculations by the villagers whether she ever had a few suitors over the years, yet for reasons better understood by her, she never showed any interest. She loved those children like her own and they reciprocated by showering her with unrelenting affection.

*   *   *

Lessie devised an elaborate bathing ritual for the children when returning home from playing. In preparation of this ritual, she would set a big wash pan of cold water out in the yard for the sun to warm. She would then proceed to strip their clothes off and wash them down in the open one by one. In one hand she would hold the kettle of lukewarm water, and in the other, her corn husk and her caustic brown soap, taking aim at the hard to reach creases where dirt collects. Franklyn would duck out on many of Lessie's primitive baths which after a scrub would leave clear skin patterns as if one had been sanded with a rough grade of sand paper and made ready for a paint job. Franklyn knew then that this was not for him. In Lessie's mind, it was an act of love. She would whip the saying "Cleanliness is next to Godliness" into them as an expression of the pride she had in her children's appearance adorned in their Sunday's best. From Franklyn's perspective, however, it was definitely an act of torture.

As far as one can turn back the hands of time, the fights between Franklyn and Lessie were ongoing and unyielding:

"Come here Franklyn; it's your turn now," Lessie's plaintive voice would be heard calling this recalcitrant boy.

"No, I'm not coming . . . leave me alone!" would come Franklyn's defiant answer.

"I said come here, Franklyn. You don't want me to come after you!" adding threat to her voice.

"I said NO!" Franklyn continues to resist.

"Boy, I said come here before I take my belt!" the first sign of Lessie's losing her patience.

"No . . . no . . . no . . . leave me . . ." stubbornly defying Lessie's threats.

"Boy, I have enough of your mouth . . ."

Lessie drops her kettle and brush, stomps her bare feet on the hard-packed earth, advances with resolute authority while her voice takes a heightened threatening sound that leaves no doubt that she's about to inflict serious damage.

> "Get your ass over here right now . . . I said, right now!!!" her voice booming, disclosing both unrestrained rage and frustration.
> "No! I said leave me alone" Franklyn throws back at her, unrelenting, escalating the confrontation.

Joy and Lennox sensing the urgency in her tone and the ominous body language; they both spring to action and corner Franklyn. They grab him by the arms and march him to Lessie, whose eyes by now are bulging from their sockets with her enlarged nostrils letting out several puffs of flaming air she gulped through her gaping mouth.

> "Ok, ok, let me go . . . let me go . . ." Franklyn finally raises the white flag.
> "Why do you have to be so stubborn, boy? See your sisters and brother don't ever give me no problem . . . get over here and keep your trap shut . . . do you hear me? I said, do you hear me?"
> "Okay; okay!"

These episodic interludes were very operatic and entertaining: this precocious, pint-sized boy with lightening fast verbal skills and the huge imposing woman exchanging words. More often, she was chastising him for his relentless provocation that could have driven her into madness. *"Ah yo Mama just don't know what ah yo put me thru" . . . Lawdy . . . Lawdy . . ."* she cries out in utter frustration. It goes back and forth until one or both get tired. It often is Lessie who grudgingly relents for another day. She would promise a whipping at some later date. These recurring confrontations, it is believed, helped Franklyn develop his dramatic flair. The only element missing was the orchestra with violins and trumpets and cymbals for accompaniment to these operatic interactions between the two, Lessie's voice fluctuating along the octave scales while Franklyn is forever teasing and telling her off. He was undeniably the defiant type. Oh, there was also much love and tenderness through all of this as well, serving as an interlude between confrontations. Here is a woman who so loves those children, washes them, feeds them, takes care of their clothes and makes sure they are protected all day long, and would readily sacrifice her life for them. All the villagers knew the depth of her commitment to them. One can never repay this debt. Deep down, it was understood that Franklyn and the rest of Olive Seales' children carry her into every aspect of their lives. Today, they experience Lessie's spirit embedded in their cells. *"She is the poetry of my soul: her passion, her caring, her love and energy are still very much part of me as they were with Franklyn,"* Lennox reminds himself. Lessie would express words when translated conveyed the message that "Hunger compels the pups to come home." She saw them as her little pups substituting what she never had, essentially representing her children. She was in a constant, perpetual state of motion around the yard: baking bakes and cod fish cakes, making a dough boy, or cooking a pot of soup, washing and ironing their clothes. She dedicated unwavering devotion to the Seales household.

Franklyn, unlike his other siblings, was uncommonly precocious, showing signs of an accelerated maturity; speaking of dreams that came deep within a fertile imagination that others found too challenging and not believable, so left him to explore his singular world. His older brother, Lennox, when asked to describe Franklyn, he would say, *"I come to the irrefutable conclusion that my brother always felt special in an almost ethereal way. He acted from his own unique perspective yet invited all to come along in the journey he envisioned. He projected a self-assurance and passionate determination that carried a price that could either inspire you or become your worst nightmare. What mattered was his opinion in all conversations that made him the center of attention. The onus was always on those who chose to listen and learn what he had to offer. One might erroneously conclude that his hubris carried a perceived insensitivity toward his listeners. To him, one had to maintain the same pace he was on or leave his company because he wasted no time nurturing you along the way. One had to keep up on this unknown destination his mind's eyes were visualizing."*

The three sisters were always in Lessie's crosshairs, checking on them like a mother hen looking after her offspring. As they matured to "young ladies," she was the one to explain the changes their bodies were experiencing. At the first sign of their menstrual period, each girl-beginning with the eldest, Joy, then Pat and finally Leslie-born two years apart would be tutored why they "bled." She would fashion a bag made out of hemp cloth for each girl in which she kept the sanitary napkins she called "diapers." They were washed after each usage and returned into the bags for the following month. This seemingly mundane exercise signified their rite of passage.

"I was ten years old," the youngest sister Leslie recalls, "when I woke up one morning to observe what looked like a red stain on the sheet that I quickly recognized as blood. The sight startled me and reacted to a sense of embarrassment. I looked closely to find more on my 'night gown,' more accurately, an old dress. I was puzzled . . . and more scared but said nothing to anyone, put my school clothes on and left home for what I thought would be another normal school day. Not more than an hour later, the teacher noticed the blood coursing down my legs and pulled me aside:"

"Do you know what's happening to you, Leslie?" she asked.

"I see blood on my leg but I don't know miss Eustace," I answered.

"Leslie my dear, I want you to go home now and speak to your mother."

"I hightailed home in a jiffy."

Lessie in the interim had discovered the stained sheet and recognized her little girl had become a "young lady." "As soon as I arrived, Lessie sat me down to lecture me on my coming of age with 'comforting words.' She took great pain explaining what was happening to my body."

"Leslie, me girl, me and you got to talk."

"What is it Lessie"?

"I'm gonna explain what happened to ya this morning"

"How did you know? You don't need to explain."

"Never mind how I know . . . yes I do need to explain young girl . . . you're just ten years old and you're a "young lady" now.

"So?"

"Now that you're having your period, I don't wanna you to have boys coming to you . . ."

"What! . . . what do you mean? No boy coming to me."

"Hear me good now. I mean that your body is changing too fast . . ."

"What do you mean, too fast . . . ? I don't understand"

"What I mean is, you're getting sensitive down there . . ."

"What? Down where Lessie . . . ?"

"Listen girl. You're gonna get all kinds of feelings, the same that boys get . . ."

"What?"

"Listen here sweetheart, don't let no boys touch you . . . you come to me if they try."

"Nobody is going to touch me, Lessie . . . what are you talking about?"

"Good, too many young girls out there getting pregnant . . . too soon."

"Oh, that's what you mean . . . nothing like this is going to happen to me . . . not me."

"Good, now, did you understand what I just told you?"

"Yeah, I think so."

"What do you mean, 'you think so'? I want you to tell me that you will do exactly what I say . . . I want you to come to me . . . ME . . . if you have any question."

"Ok, I will Lessie . . . but tell me something . . ."

"Tell you what?"

"How come you don't have children, Lessie?"

Lessie rolls her eyes. "Look . . . young lady . . . I'm not talking about me."

"I was just wondering Lessie . . . how come?"

"Some people have children; some don't"

"Ok, how come you don't have any?"

"I just told you . . ."

"Explain to me, why."

"I have nothing to explain . . ."

"Ok . . . ok"

"Look baby, if you have any questions, come to me . . . you understand?"

"I understand, Lessie."

"Give your mama a big hug sweetie."

"Good girl. Now promise me, you hear, promise me that you'll run to me if a boy tries to bother you."

"They won't bother me."

"I said promise me."

"I promise, Lessie."

Lessie's lessons guided my decisions as I matured into adulthood, to keep my promise until I was ready for marriage eleven years later and raise my own family. Us three girls, now married and grandmothers, love to spend time reminiscing the lessons learned, and to recapture the joy of growing up with Lessie."

LABOURNE STREET

Years had already passed when it was discovered, while reminiscing about their upbringing, that the family house was on "Labourne street." This would be insignificant taken in the context of the childhood days, however, as toddlers; there were no street signs anywhere in the village. Urban planning concept was not one that had entered into the lexicon of the early settlers. Location of a given house was done simply by pointing to a direction before proceeding to a destination. However, when Franklyn was six years old and Lennox was ten, two city workers in their truck drove to the village. Their presence attracted immediate attention from the residents. The children, as customary, were drawn to whatever seemed to disrupt their routines and surrounded the workers.

"Don't move any closer . . . back up;" a worker shouted a warning command that was heard by all.

They were observed taking out their pick axes and proceed to dig a hole in which they erected a wood pole with a sign that read Labourne Street. This trifling, one might say, development marked one small step toward modernity. The villagers, henceforth, could begin to claim an identity in the context of neighboring villages. Visitors could point to the sign and trace their way to a designated destination. It gave the residents a certain character that was heretofore missing. The children were not cognizant of its impact on their lives; however the old timers were very proud of their new found identity.

Adjacent to the Seales house was a stone building. It consisted of one large open room with a stage at the front entrance, two closets, one to the right of the stage and one to the left, a front and a back door, and windows to the front, rear and sides. A few benches and wooden chairs were strewn around the room. Everyone in the area referred to it as "The Lodge." It was a community center that provided multipurpose services to practically all of the kids who would take refuge in the Lodge on many occasions to fill their empty hours and days. Words would go out quickly from house to house that Franklyn had arrived at the Lodge, and the young girls would join him to play a variety of games, or acting out some imaginary parts. He possessed a certain magnetism that attracted them to him. Little did we know that the Lodge was his first laboratory. He was a Philogynist without knowing it.

There came a time when everyone referred to it as the "Society Lodge," a place where members of the local credit union stopped to make their weekly deposits. It was also a place for socials: a school room for early childhood, a dance hall, a place for political rallies, and a myriad of activities in either small or large groups. Often times, Lennox would play on the steps of the Lodge where he would walk his little brother and play marbles and teach him how to spin a top. The Lodge was, for all intents and purposes, part of their playground. It was also the place where they first encountered a bat. Those bats had staked their living quarters in the rafters of the Lodge that offered them protection during the daylight hours only to fly away and disappear in the darkness of night. Many boys in the village would take pleasure chasing the bats out of the room, those whose radar might be temporarily impaired. They played in front of the building also which served for Franklyn's outdoor performances but not before bringing flowers and creating the backdrop for his play. The children from the neighborhood would linger on the steps in the early afternoon breeze to watch young Franklyn entertain them. The building also had a path for marbles and spinning tops. It was not unusual to call the Lodge their sanctuary, their Zeitgeist. They would play until they felt hunger pains that called for Lessie's food.

Labourne street was the neighborhood playground from the beginning, looking across the street from the Seales house to the communal pipe, the public pipe where villagers without running water were able to come and fill their metal containers, share community gossips, and go home. Yes, Franklyn Vincent Ellison Seales was born in the house on Labourne street in Calliaqua and Calliaqua was never the same. The boy was traveling at the speed of light and everyone felt his 'light' despite the fact that few truly understood the significance of the gift with which he had been blessed. Big brother had to grow into his light. Paradoxically, Franklyn always acted as if he had them all figured out and well scrutinized, and that he deciphered what made them tick. Lennox was always taken by Franklyn's compulsion to be right.

He was what people generally called 'stubborn.' Much later, Lennox realized that it was not so much his stubbornness than the energy force that drove him to improvise and act with a certain absoluteness. He was not the typical compliant child. He instinctively knew what he liked and disliked. Their mother would often find herself corralled in a tug of war with him. Those conflicts were triggered by his demeanor that revealed a certain 'knowingness' she found difficult to get a handle on, a challenge she did not experience with her other children. In the West Indian culture, people call this type of behavior as "own way." In the halls of academia it is referred to as "oppositional defiance." He knew what colors, foods, clothes and most everything else that pertained uniquely to him. He knew what turned him on and off instantly. Retrospectively, one might be lead to conclude that it was foretold. Not one to mince words, he worked with his thoughts as if they were driven by this non-quantifiable super energy.

Franklyn was simply marching to the beat of a different drummer. Over the years and since his death, one came to accept the notion that he was a visitor sent on a brief mission. As they were growing up, Lennox concluded that Franklyn never identified with lack or limitations. He was the first "no-limit-person" that he has ever encountered. He simply despised lack in anyone he met, mostly, their mother. She would moan and cry about her status ad nauseam. He, however, developed the ability to insulate himself from her unending lamentations to not only ignore but summarily forget them because he considered her state of mind a distraction he was unwilling to encourage. He never empathized with anyone who embraced poverty, regrets. One surmised that Franklyn and Lennox were fundamentally different in that respect. Lennox wholly identified with his mother's plight and often made suggestions about how she should endure her challenges. Franklyn ignored her with unconcealed contempt. he came to believe after long examinations of his mom's episodic outbursts that Franklyn was not unerringly insensitive, but knew innately that embracing poverty or any condition of lack would create more of the same, transforming it into a self-fulfilling prophesy, something that he vigorously rejected. He learned this early from Franklyn and he also had to forgive him for the persona he detected in their earlier development. Once he reconciled the fact that they were on a different path, it became easier to love him more and to accept that he was not of the same consciousness with any of them around him. His brain did not operate in a manner that corresponded to the real world as one knows it. He was an unassailable force that exacted a linear path.

There came a time when Franklyn began to learn about the value of money, and Lennox designated himself to be his teacher. They played a game that he devised to activate Franklyn's learning process. The object of the game was to play with coins and to cover a small coin with a larger one. A simple game governed by rules that Lennox concocted. Franklyn had what the natives would call dimes which were the smallest of the coins, or what are called now ten cents. Nickels or five cents were larger in circumference, and pennies were as big as two shillings or fifty cents. One cent was smaller than a penny or what is called two cents. Stay with me . . . Lennox would often trick him by using his nickels to cover Franklyn's dimes and convincing him that the bigger coin was the more valuable, thus taking his ten cents with his five cents. Eh! It's survival of the fittest, as far as one is concerned.

"Franklyn, let's go play our coin game," Lennox suggests, inviting him to display the pocket change he kept in his trousers.

"Show me your coins" I say.

"Ok," he says.

"Put them all on the ground and count how many you got. I'll do the same with mine," I say.

"Ok," he says.

"See, I have eleven coins," I say.

"I have six," he says.

"Now, Franklyn, remember for each bigger coin I have, I can "eat" your smaller coin, because it's worth more and can buy more with it, ok, you understand me . . ." I ask?

"Yeah . . . but, five of my six coins are small . . . and . . ." he says.

"Ok, let's start. Put your coins down," I say, interrupting him. I don't want him to think too fast.

"See, my bigger coins cover all your five smaller coins, so I win again," I say.

"What!?!" Franklyn exclaims, befuddled.

Their sister Joy who is playing nearby saunters over.

"What are you guys doing?" she asks.

"Mike (Lennox's more familiar name) told me my small coins are worth less than his big coins and he won . . ." Franklyn says.

"Wait . . ." Joy pipes in.

"Go back! Go play with the girls . . . we don't want you here," Mike barks at her.

"A dime is worth more than a nickel, Franklyn," she says.

"Huh, but my nickel is bigger and I covered the dime with it." I counter.

"You're cheating, Mike" my sister retorts.

"I was busted . . . It didn't take long after Franklyn became my apprentice that he caught on to my deception and that was the end of the game, thanks to my sister whom I temporarily hated."

As mentioned, the Lodge was the venue where they played and continued to learn about life. Lessie would often set her coal pot outside the rear of the Lodge. When afternoon came, she would roast corn, cook a fish soup, fry fish, and make tea. She had a very peculiar yet not singular habit among the locals that made the kids come to a temporary halt from their usual activities. She would never walk to the bathroom to urinate. As their eyes traced her walk, she would proceed to the opposite end of the wall, raise her leg and empty her bladder on the side of the building. They would burst into laughter, but with the years that passed they grew accustomed and thought nothing of this strange and unladylike habit.

There comes a time in every family in the neighborhood when it is of the utmost importance to attend to one's physical wellbeing by giving mother nature a helping hand. On a Saturday of every three months and sometimes more frequently as the situation demanded it, Lessie would gather the Seales children outside in the yard and motion them one by one to get inside a large pan filled with water; each would be given half of an orange to hold; then she would conduct her ritual by administering each one of them a dose of Castor oil. They unfailingly dreaded her call that signified time had arrived to swallow a spoonful of the yuckiest substance man could have invented and market in a bottle. The putrid smell was enough to repel a skunk, yet was destined to go into their mouths, down their esophagus, deposited into their stomach, slither through their intestines where it would flush out the putrefied food that remained in their guts, perhaps for days. Franklyn once again as expected would present the greatest challenge. After chasing after him around the yard, the sisters and big brother would restrain him by grabbing both of his feet while Joy and Pat held his arms. He was not easy to handle. He kept on trying to pull away from them, but he was one against three. They had the advantage albeit a slim one at that. He was like a wild grunting piglet facing a pending execution. Lessie with one hand would force open his gnashing teeth and with the other slip the spoonful of that dreaded oil, quickly drop the spoon and with both hands forced his mouth shut until he swallowed it. As they let go, he would scream at the top of his lungs, stump his feet and run off into the house only to dash out for the latrine at the far end of the yard. This was a remedy that she practiced unfailingly to purge their 'sour system' after eating an excessive amount of fruits especially mangoes, a staple in their diet.

As one who lacked adult maturity of everyday things, Lennox (Mike) would defer to Lessie's caring and devotional dedication for their wellbeing and do his best to show the respect she so richly deserved. Franklyn by contrast would deliberately taunt her by asking pointed questions:

> "How come you don't have a man coming here to see you, Lessie?
>> What's the matter Lessie, don't you like men?"

This would result in dramatic displays of passion and fury. Lessie was also as dramatic in a very primitive way. Instead of fetching the strap to spank him, she would raise her voice a few octaves and proceed to chastise him verbally:

> "I will get you boy . . . I swear . . . just let me get my hands on you . . ."

Her carotid arteries were visibly throbbing, triggered by this young boy's temerity. Her almost predictable reaction had very little or no impact on getting Franklyn to be respectful or tolerant. In fact, her strategy would fuel his aggression to provoke her more and earning him her promise to give him a good spanking. It was very uncommon for her to eventually, after reaching the end of the rope, mete out her revenge because Franklyn displayed a certain quickness in his footwork and wasted no time to flee the scene. Lessie would always threaten to tell their mother about his irascible behavior. Franklyn showed much indifference and proceeded to walk through the fire of life with an energy that was unstoppable.

On many afternoons when it rained, they all sneaked into the Lodge where there was an old piano on the stage at the entrance of the building. The rainfalls carved mud puddles in the yard and the potholed streets had become ponds that made them dance joyfully, defying Lessie's call to return inside the house. One would invariably find Franklyn on the stage surrounded by the girls playing some game he would improvise. He often used whatever was available as props for his productions: old clothes completely worn out, tin cans, wooden sticks etc. They nonetheless had no clue that deep in the recesses of his being he always held a strong vision of performing before large audiences. In retrospect, there's no mistaking that Franklyn was blessed with talent, the will, the ambition, the drive to dream. He was unstoppable. It did not matter whether it was a fight with Lessie or directing the area kids in a play or some imaginary game. He had it in him to vent out.

All knew of Franklyn's fondness for cats and long observed his intermittent wheezing, so without seeking the benefit of a medical opinion, Lessie concluded that her boy was asthmatic. An old lady, a friend of Lessie's who lived in the area, when word got to her of Franklyn's apparent affliction recommended a remedy she claimed was 'full proof' because it was passed down from her grandmother's side of the family tree for generations-more than likely based on folklore. She recommended that

Lessie prepare a soup in which she would boil a lizard, yes, a lizard-the kind that meandered aplenty in the yard, brown or green didn't matter-and to give it to Franklyn at lunch time. So said, so done. Lunchtime came and one can hear Lessie yell: "Franklyn, oh, Franklyn . . ." Unbeknown to the 'patient,' he drank the soup without a whimper, smacking his lips as he gulped the entire bowl. However, contrary to her friend's assurance of its efficacy, the remedy did not work to Lessie's chagrin. Undaunted and doubting her own execution of this brew, she decided to boil two lizards at one time for double potency, yielding the same disappointing result. Nothing worked even after several trials. The children were oblivious whether he ever discovered Lessie's trickery. Much later upon his arrival to America, Franklyn consulted a doctor who diagnosed that his wheezing was triggered by his close proximity to cats. He was allergic to cats. Problem solved, or was it?

On one side of the Seales house lived Ms. Joyce and her daughter, Margaret. She was an only child, and Ms. Joyce was very protective of her only offspring who was much older than all of them. Margaret loved to flash her dazzling smile of pearly white teeth that one could hardly not notice. She would cross the street over to the house to play with the older sister, Joy. On the other side of the house was Mrs. Gibson, who had five children. The Gibson family was what euphemistically called "St. Vincent Whites." She was the mother of three boys and two girls, all older than Franklyn and Lennox. The boys had mechanical skills. Mrs. Gibson operated a grocery store but did not sell liquor, one of the few that did not. She was the preferred little grocery shop. It attracted every resident that lived around the neighborhood. It was the place where one's mother would send you to buy a pound of sugar, a pound of flour, tea bags and coffee. It also was the place where if a family could not afford to buy cash, she would gladly extend credit until the money came in. So people felt a real kinship with Mrs. Gibson for the unforeseen tough times. Her husband was a telephone man who was killed tragically on his motorcycle; his widow became the lone caretaker of their five children. She was not only one of the local shop keepers but also a social butterfly. She entertained the men as well as the women in her shop. She was the local nurse or 'first responder' when a youngster would fall from a tree or from a bike. They all went to Mrs. Gibson to be 'patched up.' She felt comfortable smoking cigarettes and playing cards with the local men at night in her shop. Another title she wore proudly was "community counselor of the social service agency for the disenfranchised," a title with no shortage of words that the youngsters hardly understood nor tried to find out the meaning.

Mrs. Gibson always kept a menagerie of three dogs and five pigs in her yard; two cats remained indoors and seldom ventured out. Every day with the exception of Sundays she could be found cooking large pots of sweet potatoes to feed her animals. The youngsters would go in the yard and eat sweet potatoes as well-not with the pigs and dogs. One could also smell the pungent aroma of Ms. Gibson's freshly brewed coffee from a block away. They all got their first taste of afternoon coffee at her house. Regardless of the problem a villager faced, Mrs. Gibson and her family were always present to help out in one way or another. So, Franklyn and his brother would go to Mrs. Gibson's to get their candy treats or whatever else they wanted at any given time. Such was her generosity. She seemingly never grew old.

There were other large families in the village, in addition to the Gibsons. The Jones were more academically minded, emphasizing school and learning. Mrs. Jones was another of those take-charge women in the area who raised her family without a husband. She was in complete charge of her offspring. No one messed around with Mrs. Jones. So, Franklyn and Lennox frequented Mrs. Jones' house where they were taught things about the world of books.

Across the street from their house was the Byron family. They were much more reserved. Lennox was, however, allowed over to the Byrons with his younger brother Franklyn, though many of their friends were forbidden to enter the yard. Mrs. Byron was very vigilant and would chase you out of her yard if she did not welcome you, jealously guarding the large number of fruit trees on her property. This did not stop Franklyn from trespassing on people's land and in their yards and proceed to help himself to mangoes, plumbs, apples, tamarind, peanuts, sugar cane, sour sop, or whatever was in season; he simply acted as if he had a divine right to people's property.

Mrs. Byron lived in a two story house. The street level portion of the house was their first classroom. Every day, mother Seales would walk her children over to Mrs. Byron along with their cousin Terry for lessons. Mrs. Byron's daughter, Val and at times Greta, would teach the

ABC's and arithmetic. Later they would learn to count and read. They were given slates to write on. This marked the beginning of their schooling.

Franklyn graduated to the Parish Hall school while big brother went to the bigger public school. He was very much an adventuresome person from the beginning. He exhibited a compulsion to draw attention to himself. As small as he was around the house, he insisted on everything that he was not supposed to have. The one thing that brought him peace and quiet was crayons. All his mother had to do was provide him with paper and crayons, and he was off to the races. He would sit and color for hours on end, and by age five, he was drawing and questioning everything.

In their still childish, immature mind, they believed they lived in a huge house. Years elapsed after migrating to America before they gained a perspective on life and returning home, they realized how small their house was. One would estimate it measured about 1100 square feet. It was their grandmother's old house where their father grew up. After he married their mother, it was a tradition to bring one's bride home. Mr. Seales, being the only boy in his family, proceeded to expand livable space to the house. He added a living room and dining room. With only two bedrooms in the house, the notion of having one's private bedroom was an alien concept to the children. To add insult to injury, not only did they share a bedroom, there were times when they had other people sharing the room as well. They had two broken down beds with worn-out mattresses that had suffered severe wear and tear. However, there was very little complaining.

Behind the house was a bath, and behind the bath was a toilet. No indoor plumbing in those days. The latrine did just fine. Franklyn, as a little boy of five, had already made claim to the front room of the house where he kept his papers and pencils to engage in his drawings. It was a wooden house like most houses in this part of town. He would draw on the boards when he ran out of paper, so the house became his original canvas. No one in the family truly knew what motivated him or what made him tick. He was so different from the rest of his siblings. He matured very early and it served to amaze and arrest all who encountered this young boy of Calliaqua.

There were not many comparisons being made among houses in the area which were built from the same blueprint. They did not have a kitchen in the house. It was built outside in a corner of the yard where there was a breeze way to it. The kitchen lacked a stove but as primitive as it was, Lessie or Pat cooked for everyone on cold pots. Often times, breakfast consisted of cocoa or tea with buttered toasted bread. They would wake up in the morning and waited until someone lit the coal pot and got a fire going. More often than not, they had a belly full of fruit before tea or cocoa. The house was not equipped with modern appliances such as a refrigerator. So there was no fridge to raid to eat leftovers. Lessie would make a dough boy or sweet bread. She would feed them, and what was left she would hide. Nine times out of ten, they would find the leftovers and chow it down. She would fuss, but soon the fussing would subside and she was right back to baking more stuff and feeding them all over. If it was a school day, they were off to school after the cocoa and the bread. If it was not a school day, they would stay outside in the yard to play. Franklyn would be challenged about brushing his teeth and taking a shower. Lessie would threaten to wash him herself. There finally came a time when no one wanted Lessie to wash them anymore. She was strong and a good scrubbing by her was sure to guarantee bruised skin. So they tried to handle the self care themselves.

Life in the village in those days was about play. The children lived outdoors. They invented games and played in the yard. With no air condition, it made no sense to stay inside the house except during torrential rains, which usually would come during the rainy season. The beach is at walking distance from the house. Calliaqua is a fishing village where most men earn their living from the sea. Some days Lessie would take them with her to buy fish. If there was a large catch that day, word would spread fast, and everyone would run to the beach to see the size of the catch. The fishermen used a large net called a "Sane". The men would cast these nets and the people on the beach would help by pulling in the Sane. If the Sane netted a huge catch, they would be awarded with enough fish for two or three meals. So, this too was a big part of how they lived. Lessie would be on her best behavior, frying and steaming fish. Jackfish was very popular as well as Robins. They ate more fish in their young lives than most people did in a lifetime. They would roast fish, stew fish, fry fish; you name it, they had it. After lunch, they were off to the beach to play and swim and eat fruits until late in the afternoon. It was never unusual to see the same people from the area do as they did. It is how they carved their never ending existence. It was all in a day in Calliaqua. They rolled home and washed up, ate more fruits, and waited around for Lessie to feed them more fried fish and bakes. The big meal on the island was lunch. One never ate a meal at night. It was tea and bakes . . . codfish and bakes . . . never a big dinner. After dinner they played outside around the lamp pole; some neighbors played marbles, and others would sit around and make believe. School nights kept them in the house doing homework and getting ready for the next day. By the time Lennox was 13, he was going to a school four miles away. Franklyn was still attending school in Calliaqua. He could walk to his school quite casually. After school, he would go over to Peggy Gibson's house and read with Tony. Weekends never found Franklyn in Calliaqua. He would undergo a metamorphosis that drove him to seek the company of the more affluent. He would trek to Villa to spend the day with the Phils family, and more often, could be found at the Minors family.

The village is located at a four mile distance from the capital, Kingstown, often mistaken by foreigners for Kingston, the capital of Jamaica. Even a mile then seemed like a rather long distance to travel by foot under a blazing hot sun, so when Saturday came, Franklyn and his brother would decide to attend a matinee at the movie house in town. As usual, they had very little money to spare to pay for a ride. Franklyn had devised a plan. They would remain at a designated intersection and hope someone with compassion would see two innocent-looking young boys wave and give them a ride. Not one to be denied, Franklyn, almost embarrassingly, would demand a ride to town from the startled driver looking at a little boy of six years of age standing defiantly in front of his car. "Move boy!" he would yell, while the sound of the horn drowned the command of the driver. Franklyn would answer by first crossing his arms over his chest and then calmly say, "Mister, I need you to take my brother and me to town . . . please!" The driver's eyes would soften and say, "Ok, jump in you two. I don't have time to waste."—It was an amazing feat to watch him operate in an adult world most of us feared to tread. To everyone's amazement, Franklyn's tactics never . . . never failed to work. They would quietly laugh it off until they reached their destination. After spending almost all they had to gain entrance to the movie theater, it was time to return home and Lennox counted on Franklyn, his brave, rambunctious, imaginative little brother to guarantee them a ride back.

*   *   *

Francis Adolphus Seales was a heartthrob of his generation with a penchant for the female pulchritude that he exploited with great success. The patriarch of the Seales clan was a rather handsome man with a charming personality and easy manners, a product of the miscegenation of the races, a legacy of the British, French, Scottish, who occupied this colony and imported African slaves to till and cultivate the land after the conquest of the indigenous Carib Indians. Francis Seales like many of his generation born on that Caribbean island bears their DNA. He was the son of St. Clair Seales, a man none of his grandchildren knew much about, except that he was of mixed Scottish ancestry. He apparently had left his wife, Lisle Elizabeth Sarsfield Lord, a direct descendant of Sam Lord, (1778-1884) one the most notorious buccaneers on the island of Barbados who amassed great wealth during his lifetime. Sam Lord's castle that bears his name was once the *it* hotel for tourists accommodations from around the world. Grandmother Elizabeth, as she was called by the grandchildren, is described as a beautiful olive skinned woman with long wavy hair that flowed down to her waist. She had three children. Francis Adolphus St. Clair, Estellita, and Athelie. Grandfather St. Clair Seales moved to America alone with the hope of reuniting with the family he had left behind to settle in Brooklyn where he became a shoemaker. Years passed and word came that he had married a local woman. His new wife would occasionally write to the family he had left home informing them of his life in America and even going as far as sending them cash, clothes and sundry items. The story goes that after his wife passed away, he moved to Philadelphia and thereafter nothing was heard from him.

Francis had missed the birth of his last son while at sea but vowed to stay close to shore. He was there, however, when the others were born. On the day of Michael's birth, he made sure to drive the three girls to town and told them the plane was bringing another brother or sister, the same routine he had repeated after the birth of his three daughters, Joy, Patricia and Leslie. On the return home, he could see that his wife had given birth to his first son on the very day the heir to the British throne was born, Prince Charles. He named his son Michael Lennox, his prince. After Franklyn's birth, my father worked at home for the government and at one time was assigned a chauffeur. Every Sunday he would take the entire family for a ride to the country side to visit friends and specifically the older sister's Godmother, Mrs. Vicky Beach. They drove along the breathtakingly beautiful mountains, the unpaved roads that cut through rolling hills and lush green pastures overlooking the ocean's green and blue colors where the shore is embroidered with foam.

When Franklyn reached his second birthday and was already manifesting a personality, though charming coming from a child, he was proving at times increasingly irritating to his mother and the other older siblings whose attention Franklyn commanded. On a day that was or should have been like any other day, the parents left the house to attend a wedding in a village nearby, and instructions were given to their oldest daughter, Joy, who was ten to keep a close eye on her brother for the few hours they would be absent. Kids will be kids. Joy was more interested in playing with the other girls in her age group than to keep a steady eye on Franklyn who as any boy would do, climbed through the window, three feet from the ground, and fell on the hardened dirt and gravel outside. Franklyn's cry for help refocused Joy's attention to rush out of the house and retrieve the badly bruised Franklyn whose tears lasted for hours on end. The parents returned home to be greeted by the youngest of the three girls, Leslie:

"Mommy . . . Mommy . . . Daddy, Franklyn fell down," she said breathing haltingly.

"What do you mean 'Franklyn fell down'?" a gruff voice is heard.

Her daddy echoed, slurring his words. He'd had a few as he always did in social company which he frequently pursued. His habit was archetypal of West Indian men who crave for the finest English whiskey and Caribbean rum infused with herbal aphrodisiacs, an indulgence they partake on weekends and days in between. Then he saw the bruises and dry blood on Franklyn's legs and shirt. Neighbors reported they heard Mr. Seales' voice bellowing his commands to Joy who became the recipient of a good woopin' that could have scarred her for life. The leather belt he had just pulled off his pants was landing on Joy's legs and bottom with skilled precision for longer than it needed to, but a lesson had to be taught. He finally stopped until tiredness had overtaken him or his arm had lost all strength, and gravitation had pulled his pants down to his ankles as the liquor took full effect. His grip around Joy's wrist loosened up, Mother then stepped up for her turn and with her bare hands administered two good slaps to Joy's fanny for good measure,

"What did I tell you . . . didn't I tell you to keep an eye on Franklyn!?!"

She was not mincing her words. Joy finally ran, sobbing uncontrollably, to the children's room, where the others cowered under the bed.

* * *

The parents' separation came as no surprise because of this lothario's chronic infidelity. It was common knowledge among the people in the village that he had several concubines, something that did not register in their young imaginations but was a well known fact, and parenthetically, is a common practice embedded in the culture among West Indian men. He fathered many children in and out of marriage. However, one could hardly say that they were solid relationships, but what one may describe as the product of his youthful indiscretions while under the influence of some adult beverages that flowed freely in the company of the opposite sex. Of all the women that one can think of, the only one other than the first wife that he genuinely cared for and remained by his side until his death, was Steph, who he eventually married and bore him four children: Dawn, Ells, Jennifer and Bridget. Years later, Franklyn's mother found companionship and the support from another man, got pregnant and their brother, Reggie, was born. Three years later their youngest sister, Debbie, was conceived. At the time, Lennox was twelve, Franklyn was eight years old. They both shared a little bedroom in the back of the house in Calliaqua.

By that time their lives were changing: mother Olive left for America on her first visit, while their father was living in Trinidad. The grandmother was left in charge, and taking care of them the best way she knew how. Lennox mused: *"I missed my mother. Franklyn, like the rest of us, was affected by parental separation; however, it did not serve to disrupt his process of creativity and drive.*

We had the small village population who knew us well, and so despite the pain we stayed glued as a result. Reggie went to live with his Grandmother Miss Cupid and Debbie went to Trinidad to live with my sister, Joy. This was a difficult passage. I was Franklyn's big brother taking care of him the best way I could. My mom would tell me that she went to America to work and help the family. Soon her letters would come with money, and I always found myself at the Post office looking for her mail. She sent several parcels of clothing and food stuff for us. Franklyn, however, never cared too much about clothes. He wore them and abused them. It made very little difference to him. In fact, nothing material mattered."

SUNDAYS IN CALLIAQUA

The sound of the church bells echoes all around. The day has come for all to gather and fellowship. Neighbors that all know during weekdays become barely recognizable dressed in their Sunday best lining the streets walking in the direction of the Anglican Church. On this solemn day, the women wear their wide brim multicolored hats. Their dresses are made by the local women who are expert dressmakers. Men wear their tailored suits made locally by the different tailors around town. It is a very formal undertaking for everyone who is anyone. It is an unplanned contest of who looks best.

There were two churches in that village: the Calliaqua Anglican Church and The Calliaqua Methodist Church. Grandmother loved her Anglican church and, as expected, encouraged the grand kids to attend. Lennox was the reluctant churchgoer. By contrast, Franklyn loved and enjoyed the old Anglican church on that hill in the center of Calliaqua. The lives of the residents revolved around the church and, all the children were encouraged to serve. As Lennox retreated from church protocols, Franklyn, however, drew closer. He became an altar boy; that seemingly gave him an audience where he fantasized drawing their attention. They were registered for Confirmation and First Communion. The minister, Father Michael, a transplanted Englishman who was assigned to the parish, fell in love with their cousin, Charmaine and soon were united in marriage. Franklyn was an altar boy who truly enjoyed his new status. He acted very pious. Years later, in retrospect, Lennox surmised that Franklyn began to answer the call to acting from his involvement at the Calliaqua Anglican Church. As an altar boy, he played his role perfectly.

They attended their church on the hill, the wonderful old stone structure which weathered many years of intense sun and torrential rain with its wonderful pipe organ, the delicate stained glass windows with detailed Victorian and traditional English antique drawings and excellent art works on the walls, some traditional and others from local artists. They loved hearing that organ sound. The self-taught organist was a gentleman by the name of Eric Alexander who was a tailor by profession who operated his own shop located in the village a few yards from the Seales home. It was on the street level of his aunt's house, while he occupied the upstairs rooms. They all referred to him by the name "Tailor," a term of endearment. Tailor was well loved by all of them in the neighborhood. He had spent time in America but proceeded to return home, once telling everyone that he wanted no part of America. His attempt to assimilate the culture was too much of an adjustment for him: "city life is fast, getting anywhere takes forever, people hardly speak to each other, and to make matters worse, the teeth-chattering cold weather caused my body to rebel," he would constantly remind his listeners. He much preferred the simplicity of home where he was a big fish in a little pond. His organ playing turned church into a festive affair that all took seriously. Tailor was not only an excellent musician but a teacher as well, willing to share his talent with the kids in the neighborhood. Franklyn became his frequent student companion, following his every step to learn as much as he could. Without fault, Franklyn would sit where the organ was located in the upstairs of the church to be closer to the music that captured his imagination and would remain there steadfastly until he was given the opportunity to become an altar server.

First Communion was a big occasion for all, as well. Both brothers took lessons in preparation for the day when they were confirmed in their white suits that were specially tailored by their older brother, Junior, who lived in Trinidad. Their father would have their suits made by him and shipped to them. It was such a big deal when their clothes arrived. They would all gather in church on Sundays, and after service they were off to Villa to go to the beach and enjoy the sea. Franklyn would often ride with Nennie and Uncle John back to their home. He would escape Calliaqua.

Many times Franklyn and his brother would hit the road for Ratho Mill to visit their aunt Emmie and her family that included their grandmother Elizabeth. Lennox would wait patiently for his aunt's bread pudding that she prepared with great love and expertise. Franklyn, however, refused to share their company motivated by his preference to visit his more affluent friends who reside in Villa. They all grew accustomed to him being away from the family. He felt ease and security with the Phils family in Villa. Lennox godmother's daughter, Barbara, was his playmate. He read books, entertained her, and played around the yard at her house; then, soon after, they were off to the beach. Franklyn had ample time to indulge in his art and his acting with her. In any event, the beach on Sundays was a great pastime for him. He also loved the security of godmother's home. By contrast, Lennox remained in the 'hood', as he calls it, with his friends, preferring to swim on the other side of the beach. The poor kids in Calliaqua hung out on Corner Bay where he went to the beach at Ratho Mill. As the days unfolded, they went their separate ways and at the end of the day, they found their way back to the house in Calliaqua. Lennox doesn't recall why or how this came about, but he gave Franklyn the nickname "Kidney." Today, it makes no sense, but back then, it stuck among their circle of friends. His little brother soon became known as Kidney by the family and close associates. Not many outside the family knew this little secret. He was rather small as a boy and he sensed therein lied the name Kidney as in kidney beans that Lessie would shell on the back steps of the house. He knew that Franklyn marched to the beat of a different drummer. There was no real strife. It was just the way it was.

They all loved Lessie's Sunday cooking. People in the village prided themselves to cook the very best meals. Along with the main course, there were elaborate fudge desserts and Guava jelly treats, in addition to sugar cakes, peanut and ginger cookies, dough boys, cakes, ginger beer and Mauby. Oh, one could smell Lessie's pots for miles. All could hear her carrying long conversations with Ms. Joyce across the yard and often times anyone who would come in from the street. Lessie guarded her pots like a pit-bull. She would make sure her "children" had that Sunday meal ready when they returned from their swimming escapades, patiently waiting to feed them. Lennox never wanted to miss feasting on Lessie's cooking. Franklyn, by contrast, did not share his enthusiasm. He did not mind dispensing with the ritual, whereas Lennox would not miss it for all the gold in the world. If Franklyn happened to be there, and it was time to eat, he would, but there was no passion, no pizzazz in it for him.

Sundays were very special in so many ways. They would eat Lessie's meals and then walk to Ratho Mill to eat their aunt's bread pudding for dessert. Lennox had to sit and wait patiently to have a slice of her delicacy. Sunday was never complete without a piece. Franklyn did not give a rat's ass about any of these family rituals. He was off running to feed his inner voice and vision. It became very obvious to them that he was driven by an image of himself that was so bright that it pulled him to listen to the voice within. He had no way to let up on the grip of his creativity. It was no ordinary grip. He was a young boy in the islands with no real role models, no one whose accomplishments in life could act as landmarks to orient him. He didn't need anyone, content to be a lone wolf with a hunger and a drive to express what was embedded in his mind, his heart and his soul. He knew innately that he had to transcend the family's limits and circumstances. He had to triumph over them and still belong. It was a highly sensitive and delicate balance.

The watering holes were ubiquitous around Calliaqua. The men of the village used Sunday after church service to while away their time drinking their coconut water laced with gin or a local brew called "strong rum" while exchanging the latest gossip, where one could find more tongues wagging than a pack of dogs inside a steakhouse, and brag about the big fish that got away. The owners of these speakeasies where rum flowed freely and in quantity constructed a rear entrance where men took their children to the backrooms of these rum shops. The children would have a 'Juicy', the local soda beverage, and watch men play dominoes and listen to them argue about local news fueled with "Mr. Rum." There were many fish stories to swap among these men with bragging rights.

They also had much fun frolicking around town on Sundays after the service. More importantly, if you were anyone of any real significance, you had to show up in church before doing whatever followed the service; however, there were those who practiced their Christian faith and used their time to help and visit the sick and the shut-ins. Franklyn by contrast was never truly interested or as passionate as his brother was in the goings on in the village. He was on a different path. He had found his niche wearing his rose colored glasses. It was a ritualistic way of being in this seaport town called Calliaqua where everything was a festival of sorts: weddings, funerals, cricket matches, child births, baptisms, and family disputes.

The villagers were a dramatic bunch that made the not-so-simple life for Franklyn so self-absorbing. There were times when two families would get into heated verbal fights that could and did turn physical. They would spill into Nanton Yard, a street that had gained a well deserved notoriety where disputes are vented and scores settled. It served as the arena that drew the villagers to witness the raw verbal exchanges that would quickly deteriorate into actual physical contacts with arms flailing every which way and occasional punches finding their target. As soon as the kids heard of the commotion, practically everyone would abandon whatever they were doing to witness the altercations between two women who were involved with the same man in a threesome that was not initially apparent to them. But once the secret was betrayed, it quickly turned into a public mayhem. More interesting were the fights between two women, one being the other woman with a married man entertaining a ménage à trois. It was not unusual to see entire families gather and verbally hash out their dirty laundry, trading the worst of insults back and forth to each other in public view, in the middle of the day and under the hot sun beating down on their heads. As soon as the word got out that a fight was in progress, the residents by the dozens spill into the streets to gawk at these verbal and very physical fights. One can draw a parallel with the times of the Romans. The "Yard" becomes their Coliseum. The protagonists are the gladiators engaged in heated full body contact fights minus body armor and swords while everyone stands on the side lines adding fuel to the already combustible arguments by applauding and egging the villains on. One can hear the spectators cheer:

"That's right Sister . . . She's messing up with your man . . . Yes . . . give it to her . . . go ahead!"

accompanied by peals of laughter and spontaneous clapping. Adults and children of all ages, mothers carrying their infants in their arms make up the reveling audience.

Franklyn was privy to all these altercations. It can be said that each of these experiences and local customs became a "teaching moment" in his dramatic development. The people took their pain and their betrayals to the street that became free drama being reenacted for the benefit of the masses. And so, one moved on to the spectator sport on Saturdays where the people of the village would show up on the lawn and the sidewalks of the streets around the Church just to witness a young bride and groom take their first walk into the sunlight as man and wife. Franklyn, being the server at many of these weddings, enjoyed the happenings. Villagers would linger on the ground and critique the bridal parties and compare them to last week's event and the week that preceded it. It is another slice of life that entertains the entire area. In addition, funerals serve the same function. They are an equally dramatic reason for the neighborhood to fuel the gossip train, gawk and witness a family burying their loved ones and also to count how many girlfriends and children would show up mourning the deceased. Franklyn and Lennox would casually select a vantage point to observe the spectacle unfolding which presented a source of great fun and laughter for many as they said goodbye to the locals in Calliaqua. Everyone loved these wakes. Attending one is like going to a party: Food, drinks, and music are de rigueur to celebrate the departed one. There are those in charge of the music while others stand up, get emotional, and dance. Fueled by liquor, the fissionable ingredient that sheds all inhibitions, it is not unusual to see some fights break out as the music plays on late into the night. No one leaves until the food is consumed and the drinkers are so drunk they can only hug the ground. Franklyn was exposed to many of these happenings, which prepared him later to deal with the classical stage. He approached it with a healthy frame of reference.

In fact, the village of Calliaqua was not unlike many others where one can find a cast of characters whose conduct enriches the lives of its inhabitants. There existed one whom everyone knew by the name of Mother James, who professed to have special gifts of healing and prophecy, and who earned herself quite a following. One would find her walking daily to a preferred location while ringing a bell announcing she had a recent conversation with God about an upcoming disaster, but more often she marched to convey the blessings that were to befall the town. Their young minds were impressionable and willing to embrace Mother James' prophecy without any prejudice. Franklyn and Lennox were always captivated by her preaching as people gathered around. Practically the entire village except for a relatively few would eagerly joined the curious, the followers, the gawkers that had complete faith in her "gifts."

"Brothers and sisters, hear me out . . . hear me good," her trembling pitchy voice rising above the noise of the crowd called out. One suspected the falsetto was added for effect.

"I'm here to bring you good news this time . . . alleluia . . ."

A whooping "Alleluia" echoes from the crowd pressing against each other eagerly expecting to hear the "good news."

"I tell you, our village is blessed with the nicest people in the whole of St Vincent . . ."

"Yeah, Mother James . . ." echoed the loud voices of endorsement arising from the crowd approvingly.

"God told me . . ." A hush descends; no one moves as they strain their necks to hear Mother James bellowing her latest pronouncement.

". . . that He is angry with the men who cheat on their wives and . . ."

"I knew it . . . that no good husband of mine . . . got to be him," a woman pipes in.

". . . and is angry at the women who interfere with married couples" Mother James continues.

"But he's been comin' to me Mother," cried the woman overpowered by guilt, as she lets out an impromptu confession.

All eyes turn on the woman who felt so righteous in her judgment a second ago who now wishes she had kept her trap shut. So, her secret is out in a moment of ill-placed moral dominance. Mother James would keep her audience spellbound for a good hour until overcome with emotions. Perhaps out of prophecies, she would walk back to her house followed by a few children.

Customarily, Mother James would attend to the sick, mend the broken and sprained bones, soothe body aches and ward off evil spirits. Truth be told, Lennox visited Mother James a few times to have a "rub down" for one reason or another: a cold, sprained ankle, sore muscles. At her 'revivals' she was what people called a "Shaker," along with the converted ones. They would watch them go under a trance and whirl into wild twists and gyrations and violent shakes and fling themselves on the ground while letting out groans that seemed to have a certain significance to them. The audiences looked at it as entertainment that filled their hours and days.

Truth be known, their presence at those meetings was not viewed kindly by the village Pastor, Father Michael, who, on no uncertain terms, condemned Mother James' influence on the faithful, calling her "an agent of the devil."

"The good Lord does not approve of your conduct," Father reminded the faithful from his pulpit.

"You practice Obeah. You are giving in to superstition, and I will not tolerate that."

To enforce his directives, he would, from time to time, either sneak around to see if he recognized any member of his church at these gatherings or send his designated emissaries to spy, all in the name of "preserving souls." Anyone caught *flagrante delicto* would be deemed an infidel and called to stand up and summarily reprimanded before the entire congregation gathered at the Sunday service. What a spectacle that was to get a dressing-down by the Pastor in front of the entire church gathering!!! Franklyn and Lennox and the other children were constantly on the lookout for Fr. Michael who would scramble his spiritual assistants to report their presence. They in turn would designate their own "security force" to alert them at the first sight of one.

Franklyn was proud to be a member of the church and enjoyed the role of altar server. He associated with many of the people who were, shall we say, 'pillars' of the church and 'defenders of the Faith,' while enjoying his new status. Since Lennox was not fixated on Church rituals he tended to stay away from the process. Franklyn by contrast was a willing captive.

They were frequently told by the guardians of the community not to step foot into certain people's yards to rifle fruits from their trees under the guise they were guarded by spirits specially summoned through certain spiritual incantations by the property owner. Their warnings were clearly designed to intimidate and control many in their small town. Defying conventional wisdom, Franklyn, even as young as he was would quickly dismiss these folks. They would take liberty to pick their fruits to send the message that they were not afraid of their so-called "spiritual powers" however, the so-called spirits challenged their imagination and wanted to know more about what they were about.

*   *   *

Mother Olive spent one year in America joining her brother, Lawrence, and his wife. During that period, her brother who had migrated to America a decade before and gained his US citizenship, did what most West Indians dreamed, being sponsored by a relative, so he filed the necessary papers that began the process that would enable her to obtain permanent residency. During that era, going to America for a "visit" was a well cultivated pretense to find work and pray immigration would not find you which could result in immediate deportation, a fate as severe as hell itself, thus ending your dream of ever entering America. It was a high stake game that was worth the peril. As she landed in America, preparation was well underway to have her do household work for a Jewish doctor on Long Island. This was the only secure work-less likely to draw attention-one could find to avoid government scrutiny. Having spent a year in America, she returned home to wait for her letter from the INS.

She moved the family to Sion Hill, where she rented a nice house and the boys attended a new school in Kingstown. *"It was great to have Mom back with us and to be living so close to Kingstown. Franklyn enjoyed this as well. We had our mother with us even if it meant that we had less money and no more gifts coming from America. We were happy. Ma renewed her focus on returning to America though, once immigration completed the paper work to secure her green card, with the promise that one day, as soon as possible, she would sponsor all of her children and we would all live together in America. Ma had Carlton, the father of my younger brother Reggie and sister Debbie, who was good to us. He was her new 'husband' and was very generous with us. He drove us in his car and gave us whatever we needed.*

Overall, we loved him and for whatever it was worth, he became the father figure in our lives," Lennox recalled.

Franklyn befriended all of the women in and around Calliaqua who had pianos in their homes. He first approached Ms. Pemberton who eventually became his piano teacher, then struck a friendship with Elsa Stevens who would teach him a little more, then he turned to my godmother, Ms. Eloise Phills. It didn't take much time for Franklyn to become her favorite. Truth be told, It was her daughter, Barbara, who was one of his closest friends. He loved to keep them company at Villa with the Punnette family where they gathered to play volleyball in the yard. Ms Phills' liking of Franklyn was merited because he kept his eyes on Barbara and reported her flirting with boys he did not approve. Barbara's denial did not convince her mother who had full faith in Franklyn's honesty and character judgment. So, to be in Franklyn's company meant that one must anticipate to abide to a degree of self-discipline. When Franklyn was not home in Calliaqua, he could also be found at Uncle John and Nennie's. He made an impression on everyone and knew instinctively how to draw attention. He possessed such a compelling personality that people became so captivated with the impression he made on them that it would last after their first encounter. As a young boy, friends, neighbors and teachers were always fascinated and intrigued. Girls of all ages loved and adored him equally. He had them following his every move. Franklyn had surrounded himself with five classmates (three boys and two girls) whom he kept close whenever the mood struck them to engage in some special, and more often than not, mischievous activities to dispel their momentary boredoms. They were Leslie, Velma, Mary, Barney, and Anthony, the latter known as "Shaggy."

In Sion Hill, he befriended the Minors family who were their neighbors and who came from the more affluent side of the track. His mother and Marguerite Minors had known each other as kids and many mistakenly referred to them as sisters. This family was well off by their standards and Franklyn was the type who was attracted to success. There were three boys and five girls who were in a position of showing him the fruits of their family's fortune in contrast to the poor girls of Calliaqua who had nothing to offer. He was by all indications a social climber. One saw his pursuit as something that afforded him the opportunity to secure the books, the crayons and many sundry items that he could not afford. For example, Antoinette had the means to buy the Mills and Boon romance novels published in Britain and very popular with the natives. Franklyn was the engine that read and discussed them and added the energy and life to the experience being meaningful.

Franklyn was unlike many young boys his age. His interests in the arts and other pursuits did not appeal to the average boy on the island. In many ways, he was considered an "odd ball." There were as many ways that he was typical as other times atypical. He much preferred the company of girls instead of boys. He drew, he painted, he read voraciously, he loved the movies and reenacted what he saw on the screen for his "audience." He kept company with people who had a certain social status in our community, people who had the toys and things that he yearned for, things he was well aware that his family could not afford. He paid a price for his association. He taught what he knew and entertained and went along with their program because it afforded him the limited opportunities the island provided to cultivate his natural born talents. He also had a strong attraction to the ocean where he loved to swim and get invited on a boat owned by a family he befriended. He spent much time walking along the beach and examining the work of the indigenous Carib artists who etched their work into rocks around Villa beach and Coronation Bay dating back several centuries before the white man discovered their island. He would study those pieces of art with great interest. Several of the pictures he drew were directly influenced by the works of the Arawak and Carib artists of generations past. In his pregnant imagination and motivated by his burning desires, he went to those rocks over and over. Amazingly enough, many people walked by those same rocks oblivious to their inherent significance, but Franklyn was the only one drawn by the mystery of these carvings and who proceeded to explore and analyze what he had found on the rocks of Villa. Each carving represented a story of the indigenous people that populated the island, descendants still living peacefully in this modern era, most clinging to their ancestral traditions, segregated in an area called Sandy Bay. He would often tell his brother how very impressed he was discovering the works of the early Carib Indian artists with whom he felt a kindred attraction. His brother was, however, nonchalant about his findings and did not connect with his discovery.

He was an excellent student who showed great reverence for classroom work. He could always be seen with a book or two tucked under his arms, learning from the written word describing a world beyond the horizon where the sea seemingly rises to meet the sky above. So in many ways, he lived a typical life in an uncommon way; doing many of the things that a local Island boy would do with an added dimension: the love of his arts and music that sustained him, drawing the attention of the locals who marveled at his unusual talents. He was known by a variety of titles: Actor, comedian, artist, dancer, hairdresser, make-up artist, fashion designer, scholar and teacher. We often wondered which title he liked best, for indeed he was multitalented. He embraced them all. The beachcomber that he was, he always maintained a great tanned complexion after spending his holidays and weekends at his godmother's house at Villa Beach. After attending a special movie showing, he often returned home to dramatize the key parts with uncanny skill and accuracy that family and friends who viewed his performances often felt that they had attended the movie theater themselves. His favorite festivals were Carnival and Christmas. Carnival was a magical time for him during which he spent many long hours at his friends' tents decorating costumes the revelers were wearing. He also enjoyed participating in "Ole Mass" so-called because it signified the day preceding the end of carnival when people would dress in inventive outfits that showcased vibrant colors and creativity. He always designed for the girls who wore his own unique creations. He kept a special notebook in which he drew designs of beautiful, extravagant evening gowns and costumes.

"We both had the light," claimed Lennox. *"We knew that anyone around us was affected by this energy of light that we carried. I had my own posse following me around Calliaqua, while Franklyn found his own retinue from the middle class girls. We always attracted faithful followers where ever we found ourselves with the company we kept. It is a gift that we were given from the day we were born. I had my crew in the hood, Franklyn had his in the 'burbs.' We both climbed out from where we were using whatever means necessary. It followed me to Brooklyn where I discovered my own inner resources of energy just like Franklyn discovered this infinite resource within. So, his networking with those girls was a two edge sword. He was of course a genuine friend, nonetheless, he saw an opportunity to get closer to the things and tools that would help him strive and become the artist he knew he was. As he grew in the world that he created, he felt compelled to bring along and teach his benefactors. These girls provided the environment for him to grow his inner spirit. He introduced them to creativeness: art, color design, creative plays. He meticulously structured life around those girls. He would go walk the beach with them and go to the Saturday matinees. He was unstoppable in his determination to escape his humble beginnings, hence was able to win everyone over by his inner vision and love. Essentially, those girls were touched and had no clue what was happening to them. There were words like "unusual" defining him. However, it was their best attempts at describing what they were experiencing and feeling. Franklyn never catered to*

circumstances in that he would create situations that would enable him to transcend the circumstance he was in. He used his inner spirit and everything within reason to rise above that which was limiting and worthless."

It was fortuitous that one day a childhood friend, Syl, gave Lennox a broken down rusty bicycle, or what was once a mode of transportation. He was nevertheless the happiest boy in Calliaqua because he had no means of getting one on his own. He had several dreams of owning one and then the dream suddenly became manifest, thanks to Syl who must have heard his prayers. It was a challenge to make it roadworthy. He saved and scrimped every dime and used his imagination and all of his limited mechanical skills to repair and rebuild the bike until he finally had it running.

They were the Whiskey family. Harold or 'Pra,' the name he was known by, was a jack of all trades. He would listen to Lennox and help him solve any problem he had. He was single mindedly anxious to get his bike fixed up, patched up and running. So Pra would allow him to use his tools and plug the holes in the tubes and tires. Hedley, his nephew, was always helpful, as well. However, he had to work with whatever projects they had before they could lend him their attention. So, exchange is fair robbery. Little by little, day after day, the bike was coming together and he lived for that moment when it would become road worthy. Living in Calliaqua, not having a bike as a young boy was like not having legs. It was crucial. So the day arrived when he made his half of a bike whole. It was painted, and each tire and tube were sound, and he was finally in business. He soon was able to show off and share his new toy with Franklyn. It became a solid point of reference for them. It was something he could share with his younger brother. He could allow him to get on it, and satisfy his eagerness to gain the confidence to ride it without falling. He was, however, experiencing a little bit of a problem following instructions, but in his typical manner, Franklyn pretended to be ahead of him in everything he was trying to convey. It was not long after that Franklyn was riding and distancing himself from his guidance following once again his inner voice and hauling ass down and around Calliaqua. Lennox can relive the joy in his brother's eyes as he rode the bike. The images of his unbridled enthusiasm were contagious. He was elated and considered it a solid accomplishment to master this skill. Then came a time when Lennox could hardly park the bike without Franklyn wanting to take it for a ride. Many times he had no choice but to tell him "NO." One day, however, he discovered the bike was not in the yard where he had left it. He hurriedly looked around and approached his sister Leslie and asked:

"Did you see my bike . . . where is Franklyn?"

"I don't know . . ." Leslie responds, shrugging her shoulders.

"Where is my bike?" His voice rises as the seconds tick . . . Two neighbors come walking by the house.

"Did you see Franklyn?" he asks restraining himself to hide his irritation.

"Ah seen him ridin' a bicycle goin' so . . ." one says . . .

"No, he went so . . ." the other neighbor said, pointing in the opposite direction.

These two cannot agree where Franklyn disappeared with his bicycle. He begins to feel the anger rising as his stomach tightens in a knot. Five minutes go by, no Franklyn; then ten, then twenty minutes. A whole hour has elapsed. What if he had dropped into one of the many potholes strewn all over the roads . . . what if he ran over broken glass and slashed the tires . . . what if he bent the rim after taking a fall . . . what if? His frustration is growing to phobic proportions when suddenly appearing out in the distance is Franklyn casually riding the bike in Lennox direction. He stops a foot away with a big grin on his face. Lennox grabs the handle with both hands, shakes it as if to wrench it out of Franklyn's hands and belts out:

"Where did you go with my bike, Franklyn? Did I tell you to take it?"

He drops his eyes to his feet then casually raises his head, guffawing

"I went for a ride . . . so?" he replied, not displaying any concern.

"What do you mean, "so"? You stole my bike without asking me and you could have messed it up."

"Nothing . . . nothing happened . . . besides, I didn't steal your bike." Franklyn answered again almost nonchalantly.

"I spent a lot of time fixing my bike and anything could have happened."

"Nothing happened . . . Mike." Franklyn's response is not what he expected.

"Yeah, nothing happened! Franklyn argued, still unrepentant.

That's not the point. You didn't tell me . . ."

"Never mind . . . Next time Franklyn, just don't take the bike without telling me" He felt his anger subsiding after concluding his bicycle was still in one piece.

Franklyn's joy ride did not sit too well with Lennox at the time; this sounds like an understatement. So they have their sibling conflicts and arguments around the use of the bike without permission. *He actually never listened to me,* explains Lennox. *He never listened much to anyone. I discovered that he had driven the bike all the way to Villa to see his grandmother.* What Lennox regarded as 'fights,' were truly not fights in Franklyn's mind. He always did rise above the ordinary. Franklyn, often times, would just measure his brother with a stare, and smile. He would not engage him, but preferred to ignore him. If he did challenge Lennox after one of these episodes, he would say, "Mike, it is no big deal." Just the idea of his brother's concerns not being a big deal would truly make him more infuriated. Yes, he was unable to get him to attend to his concerns but he could not accept him walking away and dismissing him. Franklyn actually saw things in true perspectives and never valued the things that others saw as worth preserving. Big brother was the one who did fret when he took the bike without permission. *"In the final analysis,"* he would say, *"we never fought per se. I fought with myself, because Franklyn would return to the house, put the bike down and be gone his merry way while I continued to vent my anger. So, I learned that he saw a future much brighter than I ever imagined."*

Franklyn placed little value on those things. He would often repeat, "Mike, no need to get upset" then move right on to his next project. By contrast, Lennox was uptight and concerned. If one studied Franklyn closely from his early youth, he never cared about material things. He placed value on some things, but for the most part, he saw things as practical and utilitarian, even personal belongings such as clothing or shoes. Bikes and other things were the least of his concerns. This attitude followed Franklyn onto adulthood and towards the end of his life. So here was a guy who was never connected to circumstances. He saw things that were bright and abundant. He transcended the ordinary in people and reacted often times with disdain. He was always attached to that which is extraordinary. So in his mind, there was no need to fight over anything material. It was, after all, only a 'freakin' bike. There were other things of much more pressing importance. He had this lofty, patrician attitude that came to him naturally. He just had something in him that allowed him to detach readily from things that were ordinary. Lennox later came to understand and to tone down his reactions because unlike Olive's other children Franklyn Vincent Ellison Seales always danced to the beat of a decidedly different drummer.

Overall, *"It was a lot of fun,"* said Lennox. He is still grateful for those moments and those times when they were able to connect and share. Despite the 'fights' or disagreements when Franklyn would be off and running with his bike, they had found a new connection. He had that part of himself that people refer to as 'mischievous.' *It is what happens when the face does not convey the intention and one discovers after the fact that the person's look and their behavior just did not correlate. "Ah! You've been had again."* Little did Lennox know that Franklyn was acting all along. Generally, they had their fair share of disagreements triggered by these frequent episodes when Lennox knew Franklyn did not know what he was talking about, yet acted as if he knew. The performer in him was always at play. On the question of clothes, he would choose one garment that he liked and wear it practically every day until it was completely worn. It was as if he drew energy and comfort from his meager supply of garments. He would rather have one good shirt that he would wear out, but to him it was all good. One has to guess that his philosophy was, less is more. There was much to learn from him in that regard. His attitude and philosophy of less being more was carried right on into his adult life. Case in point: when he became a man, instead of buying three sweaters for $100, Franklyn would rather buy one for $100. He had very little clothing for this very reason. He would buy the best of everything, from food to clothes. He never wanted more. He was a minimalist before most people knew what the word meant.

To say that Franklyn was a precocious child is an understatement that everyone would unanimously confirm. Clearly he possessed God-given gifts that became manifest at a very tender age to the amazement as well as the consternation of his siblings, his peers and adults alike. Long before he reached his teens, he showed a keen interest in the arts nurtured by his imaginary flights of fancy that he described to his listeners who were captivated by the images he painted. Whether they understood him or not did not matter. He had his audience willing to come along on that imaginary ride. Even then he had certain characteristics that were distracting and bordered on the dramatic. He was acting without a script. He was perceived by some as cute and by others, dramatic, and then by others as acting too girly. So, his sensitive tendencies were manifesting profoundly. By the age of 6 it was obvious to big brother that he was displaying much of his sensitive side, not an uncommon trait among creative people. Now, being born in the Caribbean, a very macho culture, young boys are forced into always denying their feelings. The focus is on being a man and being in charge. Franklyn played some typical games that would be construed as girly games, such as rope jumping. In the Caribbean at that time girls enjoyed jumping rope. In addition, he played jacks, but there again some boys would play with the girls to gain their attention. He also played some of the male dominant games like spinning tops and marbles. Franklyn's entourage of friends comprised mostly girls who were very enamored of him. He knew the neighborhood guys, but gravitated towards girls more so than with his gender.

So, one could easily dismiss thoughts and attribute behaviors as a deviation from the macho male dominant culture and not just a display of femininity. In retrospect, Franklyn acted much more feminine when we were younger. He was not interested in weightlifting, sports or typical boyishness, boxing, cricket or climbing trees. He was a sensitive guy. He was into his art, drawing and playing with the young girls versus the boys. After he arrived in the United States, he behaved and conducted himself in a way that would hardly be considered feminine. The outward sensitive behaviors went away or at best were suppressed.

He moved from Parish Hall School to Calliaqua Public School at age 5 and left at age 7. After moving to Sion Hill, he attended Richmond Hill School in Kingstown. Their father would tell Lennox over and over as a child that he was a 'prince.' He did not at first grasp the significance of the title he chose to confer on him. A prince of what? He understood a prince had dominion over his subjects like his namesake Prince Charles, but whom did he lord over? He finally came to believe what his father was saying and stayed humble with the knowledge that he was chosen to help people manage and untangle their jumbled emotions. He saw Franklyn as a prince as well. He had a gift to take people out of their mundane existence and transport them into a place in the beyond. He had what the French call, a "Je ne sais quoi," in other words, *he had an indefinable quality that makes somebody or something more attractive or interesting.* In St. Vincent, he would demonstrate this energy, this indefinable quality, by any means possible. His friend, Valerie, would tell them that Franklyn would visit their home to play the piano. Her mother would comment over and over, "were it not for Franklyn, that piano would never get played." She was annoyed that Val and her sister did not play or take advantage of the piano. The only time it was used was when Franklyn appeared at their door. So the Mama threatened the kids that she would give the piano to Franklyn since they did not appreciate nor simply show an interest in music. This was typical parenting psychology in the islands. It was the Mother's way of trying to motivate the children to do what they simply had no interest in doing. As in, *"If you don't appreciate it, I will give it away, get it?"* However, kids like Val appeared to be distracted whereas Franklyn was always in the moment, always connected to all of the gifts that God gave him. *"God saw him coming and he poured a bucket full on him."* Lennox would say. Franklyn embraced it all and was off running: Always oppositional but always centered and connected to what he wanted. His inner visions drove his 'bus.' They had no real way of understanding all of this at times, so he was considered the odd ball. In fact, he was *on the ball,* which they later discovered. Oh boy, was he ever on the ball!

So, here again is another archetypal example of how he would develop these friendships that allowed him access to things that were not available in his own environment, and as a result, he would educate and teach these idle girls about the meaning of things. He possessed a beautiful soul and took this inner love wherever he was. Lennox had many conversations with Franklyn because he would often get angry with him for his friendships with those who were from a lower station that he believed stifled his development.

The year 1960 came in a rush, and life began to change dramatically for all of them. Mother Seales received word that her immigration papers were finalized and that she was granted permanent residency in the United States. She was on her way back to the States for the second time, as a permanent resident: the promise of a new day for the Seales family that would bear fruit in the years to come. Leslie remained in the care of the Minors family who had three boys and five girls of their own. Once their mother left for the States, they were left in Sion Hill to scramble but life there was becoming too much for them. They made one other move while their mother was in the states, this one to Fountain. It cost more to rent, but they needed more room. They rented a bigger house in Fountain on a big spread of land, close to the river where was an abundance of fruit trees. It was interesting, a change for the better. Franklyn and Lennox attended the neighboring school. It was a time of transition for the rest of the family. By that time, the second sister, Pat, was a mother as well. They had moved to a big open house with lots of space for all to run around, however they soon realized that they were better off in Calliaqua. So once again, they moved back to their roots and their house. It was cheaper to operate, and they could call it home. The house was paid for and despite the size, they made it work for all involved. So Fountain School was limited to about one school year tops. Franklyn was all dressed up in his uniform going to Kingstown Grammar School. He would wear his khaki shirt and pants; he looked so well in his outfit. Lennox went to St. Martin School when they wore blue short pants and white shirts, but there were times when they wore long blue pants and white shirts. It was learned much later that Ms Phills who regarded Franklyn as a son seriously considered adopting him with both mother and father away from the roost. Mama Olive evidently had other plans for her son.

Carl Sherwood, a native of Trinidad, was in a loving relationship with the oldest sister, Joy, while he was in St. Vincent. They lived on Sion Hill. Joy moved to Trinidad after her daughter Jemma was born and after she had met the man whom she eventually married. Jemma had turned two when Joy followed Carl. The youngest of the sister, Debbie, who was two years older than Jemma, would join them much later.

Mother Olive had made them a promise that one day the family would reunite in America. That hope sustained them month after month that stretched into years. Franklyn was only eight years old without a mother while their father had moved to Trinidad and Tobago. He found steady employment at the Pointe-à-Pierre oil refinery located in the area by the same name once inhabited by the Spanish conquistadors who called it "Punda de Piedras" or "Point of Stones" and were attracted to its scenic beauty and rich soils. The French later arrived on the island in 1783 and translated the name to "Pointe-à-Pierre." The area gained so much popularity after the arrival of the French that the population increased from 290 in 1797 to 846 in 1812. In the intervening years, it grew to become one of the most important refineries in the western hemisphere. By the time my father found work at the refinery in the late 50's, it was big business that attracted hundreds of workers from neighboring islands where work was abundant and well-paying.

They had temporarily lost all physical contacts with their parents but still felt loved and protected by their extended families in their little village. Their father sent them letters with money and mother did the same. Packages of clothes came from their mother. Pat with her new born son Andy, Franklyn and Lennox were a contented bunch that leaned on one another to grow very quickly without the strict parental supervision normally found in a two-parent household. Their sister, Leslie, who was left in the care of the Minors would visit the house regularly to spend the day. How much of an impact their parents' absence played in Franklyn's psychological development is impossible to measure accurately, except to say that he, like all of the other children, did not feel a sense of abandonment that would theoretically be brought on first by the dissolution of their marriage and secondarily by their geographical relocation. Franklyn had found a way to isolate himself by compartmentalizing his emotions which enabled him to function at a higher level than all of his contemporaries. There were moments of grief that Lennox would experience as a result of not seeing his parents. There were people around but no real substitute for a mother and father being there. Everyone on the island knew the expression, "Making do," so they rolled with the punches and bought into the hope that one day their mother would get them to America. It always seemed like forever. In the meantime, life in Calliaqua went on and the two brothers lived in the way it was. They accepted that Lessie was always on standby and would guard them and protect them. She was the ultimate guardian who would not hesitate to lay down her life for them, and the villagers knew this too well which explains the respect everyone showed her. She loved them dearly and shared everything with them.

ADRIFT BUT NOT ALONE

A year had passed since the family matriarch left for America. Leslie, who was staying with the Minors family, left for Trinidad to join the eldest sister, Joy, and her daughter, Jemma, in anticipation of a letter informing her to report to the American embassy in Trinidad. Leslie's voyage to Trinidad was aboard the Carib Clipper owned by their mother's relative, Ruel King who ferried passengers to neighboring islands. Her departure was scheduled for 8:00 AM and she proceeded to stop in Grenada to pick up passengers then for the final leg, Trinidad, pulling into the harbor the following early morning hours.

The year was 1956. *"I had lost my youth when my parents split up,"* Lennox reminisces. Barely eight years old, his mother would often confide her pain to him. By listening to her complaints day after day, weeks after weeks that stretched into months and years, he began to learn ways of recognizing and interpreting specific causes of her state of mind. He was present to listen and try as best as he could to give her a degree of reassurance, to help her cope with the struggles that brought her these psychic torments. By the age of twelve, he already knew too much and too early the game of life. Franklyn was isolated from this assault on the psyche while Lennox ran straight into it, at least not consciously or by choice but rather by circumstances that were beyond his immediate control. Intuitively he sensed that there was something within that enabled him to assuage his mother's concerns. Franklyn somehow developed in a very diverse way; consequently, today Lennox became a Psychotherapist helping people to deal with whatever takes them away from ease, peace and their authentic selves. This learning curve began with his mother and her being his first patient.

Their mother was very protective of them. They both tried to circumvent her overbearing protectiveness. Lessie on the other hand was more trusting of the process of letting them go face their daily existence. Their mother was also very melodramatic, always preoccupied about them catching a simple cold and worrying needlessly about life. Lennox surmised that her condition must have been "congenital." She lost her mother during her early childhood and that set the stage for a certain amount of neurotic underpinnings. She worried about all things and everything because she lacked the firm support from her husband in the manner anticipated in a married relationship. Their father neglected to readily give her the necessary support she needed that would motivate her to be a strong individual. She was strong nonetheless without ever fully recognizing her inner strength. She never dwelled on sickness. Mother Olive was a doting one much too cautious about a lot of things and acted as if her children would melt if exposed to life vicissitudes that daily confronted them. It was not a good recipe for young boys in St. Vincent. Life was tough and difficult, and they needed to face pain without being subjected to her relentless protective shield. Lessie by contrast served to introduce them to the fires of life and the pains that accompany this life without much fanfare. Lessie, to them, knew better. The symbiosis served to mold them into the people they became. She was permissive and would run interference with their mother about their survival skills. So yes, mother Olive was caring and protective; though caring and loving, was much too hands on; that triggered their resentment and rejection of her approach, but Lessie was daring and raw.

Despite their mother's departure, their lives, their neighbors and the village at large continued to ebb and flow along the same predictable routines. Mondays came after a long tiresome weekend of fun and more fun with their friends to face school work. They were up as soon as a shaft of morning light pierced thru the latticed window signaling school bells were beckoning them. They had to face the cold shower in the open four by four bathroom which was basically a series of cement blocks built in the yard without the benefit of a roof and with a rickety door that gave them minimum privacy. A lead pipe precariously held against one cement block by a rusted nail provided the water for their shower. They took turns to take their daily cold wash. A hot water pipe was not a commodity known in the overwhelming majority of homes, practically non-existent. It was in fact an unknown amenity with rare exceptions reserved for the elite class of the island. After putting on their school uniforms they would wait for Lessie's tea, cocoa and toast with butter. She would also throw in some guava jelly and some fried jack fish left over from the day before. Fruits were abundant and completed their breakfast to hit the road for the mile walk to school. When lunch time came around midday, they walked back home to eat more fish, plantains, sweet potato and some vegetables. School ended at three which meant play time for all of them. Some would venture to the beach for what they called a "dip" and watch the sun go down. Their Saturdays began early and were divided between the beach and catching a matinee viewing at the movie theater.

The months ticked away one by one until one day, a year after their mother's departure, a letter arrived bearing the much anticipated good news that Leslie's papers were approved to migrate to the United States to join her.

"What about us," Franklyn and Lennox inquired.

They were told that Leslie was the first scheduled to make the trip to America, a dream wished by all their friends. They were also reminded that they would soon hear from their mother. Leslie's passage was booked to leave on July 15, 1961 the very day of Franklyn's birthday. Leslie received the news with much anticipated relief but with mixed feelings, contemplating the separation from her siblings that overshadowed her reunion with her mother. At the tender age of fifteen, she boarded a Pan Am Airlines plane for the non-stop flight to JFK for a new beginning. She arrived in New York and was greeted by her mother and Carlton who drove her to a house on Gates Ave in Brooklyn owned by Mrs. Cambridge, a childhood friend of theirs. She had migrated to New York several years before and established herself quite comfortably. Leslie recounted her good fortune stemming from her passion for "playing the numbers." With her considerable winnings she bought the house on Gates Ave, another one on Quincy Street, another on Pacific Avenue and yet another on Washington Avenue. She converted them into rooming houses that she rented out to new immigrants from her native land. One could convincingly say that Mrs. Cambridge had achieved the American dream cherished by all immigrants.

When their mother left on her second trip to America to receive her permanent residency, Franklyn and Lennox were living on Sion Hill. Two of their neighbors were Murray Seales and his wife, Elise, and their two children, Freddy and Jennifer. On numerous occasions their father told Lennox that Murray, though they shared the same last name, may not be related to them. He believed they were of a "different branch of the Seales lineage" from a "separate blood line." Born on such a tiny island colonized by Europeans, they shared not only the same name but most likely the same DNA going back several centuries. Lennox found his explanation rather surprising because Murray bore an uncanny physical resemblance to them. (To foreigners like me who visited St Vincent, I found the resemblance among many natives very eerie.) Murray on the other hand always accepted them as family. He was a real go-getter. He worked hard at whatever he had to do, which brought him financial security. He built a beautiful home overlooking the bay where one has a clear view of the planes landing at the island's only airport. A sister, Stella, product of another liaison, years later bought land adjacent to his on which she built a house as well. Murray died a few years ago. His children, they were told, migrated to the U.S. and live somewhere in Brooklyn. [As we are documenting these memories of their childhood, news came that his son Freddy passed away in May 2010 after a long illness.]

After their mother's departure, life was bitter sweet in many ways. There was hope that one day they would all reunite in America. On the one hand, there was the longing for her which seemed to take an eternity before they could see each other again; on the other, there were friends and school and things that occupy their minds but nothing truly enough to fill the void of not having a mother around. For Lennox, these were moments of grief and sadness. With Franklyn being younger, it was a challenge to fathom his inner feelings. No one could penetrate the invisible psychic wall he had built to isolate himself from the mundane. Outwardly, he appeared to be okay. He played with Freddy and Jennifer and continued to draw on everything including the walls in the house.

Franklyn was eight years old and Lennox was twelve, awakening one morning by the usual sound of the cock crowing but surrounded by an unusual stillness in the house. They came to the realization that they were on their own, left to steer their own ship through the ever changing waters of life; calm at times but with swift treacherous undercurrents. Franklyn remained true to his heart delving into his inner callings. He displayed a certain seriousness as he acted out different roles with a girl who lived across the street from them in Calliaqua. She knew her as Marge. She became the leading lady he directed and acted with at the Lodge. Today, the word "slumming" could define the environment. When Franklyn was at Lodge, he was slumming. Lennox was convinced that he would prefer to be down in Villa and Indian Bay with the girls with money and stuff. However, he had his days in the Lodge playing different roles with his friend. It was all about his becoming. He continued to perfect himself no matter the circumstances. Looking back into that dusty, funky Lodge, he saw it fit to make believe, to act out characters he invented. In the words of the poet T.S. Eliot: "*We shall not cease from exploration. And the end of all our exploring will be to arrive where we started and know the place for the first time.*" It was understood that experience teaches wisdom. If one travels from a starting point, one will come back to that point with more depth, more capacity to understand and see things in different ways. So one's perception of where one began will be different because of all that one has been through in the mean time. And, Franklyn will be able to understand perhaps why he left his environment in the first place. He will be able to understand the role he played there and the importance it played in his life. He was released to the highest state of creativity and capability. It was all about the human stage and realignment.

He was always living what Nature had so generously placed within him. Little did anyone know that one would see Franklyn dressing up and putting on makeup. None dared question his motives, because one truly believed he was realigning with what the spirit was driving him to do. It was not about the makeup or the dressing up, as much as it was about the "gift." Franklyn knew who he should be. It came to him at a tender age and he held onto the vision no matter what. He knew what he liked and he protected and defended it with not much afterthought. He also knew who he was not. He had an innate, unmistakable understanding of who he actually was. One would visually scan their house in Calliaqua that was so simple. There was not much of anything: a two bedroom wooden house covered with a galvanized tin roof that needed frequent changes once rain water had rusted the metal and punctured the holes that let water drain inside the rooms, over-looking the unlit narrow potholed street where many of the villagers trekked on their way to work or to the church on the hill. There was never an abundance of anything material. They had Lessie's spirit there with them and the energy of the food she cooked and the lessons she taught. Yes, Lessie was always lecturing Franklyn and Lennox. In the absence of the parents, she knew they needed guidance and was giving them her best of what life taught her. Franklyn, however, had an answer for everything, showing her no respect. He would make comments that were very personal and hurtful. Lessie's smile revealed her bare gum where teeth should be, so Franklyn would hurl crude jokes by calling her "skull," a name that surely evoked pain. One time they all heard him say, "Lessie, when I can get some money, I promise to buy you some teeth." His comments would draw laughter from his friends; nonetheless, Lessie would remain just as sweet and giving to him the next day.

Lennox had no clue what unconditional love was about, however, Lessie was an angel and a champion to them, the personification of the purity of the human spirit. Sometimes when one reflects on the suffering of young people today, broken homes, school dropouts, abusive parents, drug addicted parents, drug and alcohol use among teens, crimes, one can readily conclude that growing up in St. Vincent and living in Calliaqua was a haven from all of the brokenness around today. They played the game of life very well. Their spirits were protected despite the fact that their parents were not with them. They were surrounded by the people of the village offering protection if and when needed. They went to school, church, they did not get involved with crime, and they certainly did not experiment with drugs and abuse alcohol except for that one episode in Franklyn's life that might have been a clue to separation anxiety that manifested itself: one day in church, during a service, in the presence of the faithful, with the villagers in a tizzy, he threw up in full view of the congregation. Amazing! Some days one has to look at Franklyn's life as a microcosm of a greater drama.

The family had moved to Fountain in a house that was bigger and older. They had good neighbors: The Griffins, Mr. and Mrs. Daniels, the Fraziers. Then down the road were two auto mechanics named Sonny Riviera, and Lloyd Bachus. They stayed around the Bachus family which comprised four daughters. The family operated a shop and owned trucks which they used to transport fish they sold in the country side. All in all, they walked up and down the strip and stayed close to these families. Their stay in Fountain was rather short and soon they were back home in Calliaqua where they felt more ease and satisfaction. They were back to living in the old house where they were born. There was a brief period of adjustment to the community and the people around. They had Lessie and Pat with her two children. Joy was gone, and Leslie followed Joy. So the boys were left with Pat and their Grandmother in Calliaqua. Lennox frequented the house where the Jones family lived. Ulric and Norris were like big 'brothers.' Lloyd was older but all look forward to him coming home after work. He was married and lived across the street. He became like a parent to them, a bright and educated man. He possessed all the signs of success on the island at the time. Franklyn stayed around the church and down in Villa with his godmother Ms. Phils and her family. So, though they lived in the same house, they daily operated in different worlds.

They could count on their father writing them his letters in which he included money and packages of clothes. Mother Olive was doing the same. They were receiving parental attention from a distance if that were even possible. They knew that there was love and caring from them, however, they had more and more freedom to drift apart and not be locked into strict parental control. Overall, they did not abuse the freedoms. They lived within certain boundaries, always knowing that people around them cared and loved them in their own way. Lennox turned to the people in the 'hood' while Franklyn turned to the more affluent who had more to offer him in terms of his own interests. Their perspectives were different. Lennox was interested in understanding the dynamics of those around him. Franklyn, by contrast, had very little interest in being trapped in his own environment. The church was in the hood which gave him a connection to the Calliaqua Anglican Church.

The Minors family had moved to the skin-charring sun of Indian Bay in a house built on a promontory, giving one a breathtaking panoramic view of the entire bay facing Young island. So was Erica McIntosh and her family. Located at less than one hundred yards from the shore, the ocean breeze blew in throughout the Minors' house and lowered the indoor temperature to a very comfortable high 70's. The sounds of the waves lapping the white sandy beachhead were a constant reminder of the tranquility of life on this island punctuated at times with laughter of children running on the beach and swimming in the tranquil waters. The night skies offered a tapestry of twinkling stars as bright as diamonds. It became a preferred destination for Franklyn to visit the family and engage in activities between him and one of the daughters, Antoinette, who was smitten by her friend's multifaceted talents and welcomed by mother Minors who adored that child as her son. Franklyn's longing for recognition and lust for acting his fantasies, colored by dashes of a dream, defined the essence of his being. Ann had the means to afford taking him to movies from where he would reenact the parts he had seen on the screen, helped with an almost photographic memory to the delight of his personal audience that he always managed to gather around him. He was displaying wisdom that defied his years.

Carnival time was, is, and always will be a very special, colorful event on this island, one which provided Franklyn a venue for his artistic talents to come to the fore by designing clothes for the girls who participated in the three-day celebration occupying center stage. His designs revealed a creativity that made his friends, among them Barbara, wonder how he could dream costumes with such unique flair. The Minors' son, Vonley, was another practical joker who loved to pull pranks on unsuspecting family members and neighbors. As his sister told the story:

> "He went to mother Olive's house. It was pitch-dark night time when Vonley put on a white sheet over his head, walked into the yard and peered through the latticed window while letting out a ghostly howl that woke mother Olive out of her sleep to see, what she believed, was a zombie-like creature invading her bedroom that nearly *frightened the woman to death*. At the time, she was pregnant with Reggie and his joke could have cost her the baby."

Vonley ran back home laughing his head off, fully energized that his prank spooked his intended victim as expected. At other times, he would 'borrow' aunt Olive's panty and his mother's bra while they were hanging out to dry on the outside line. Now, these two women had, like they say, 'meat on their bones', hence were exceptionally large, and consequently wore oversized underwear that looked enormous on a little boy's body frame. The sight of him wrapped in these garments never failed to draw peals of laughter from the neighbors. One evening, both Barbara and Leslie decided to go in the yard to wash clothes against their better judgment, and after being told by mother Minors that it was too dark, it was too breezy and cool, to leave things for tomorrow morning. Vonley and his friend, Larry McCauney, heard the conversation and decided to teach these two girls a lesson. They both pulled a white sheet over their heads and held a small flashlight in their mouths. As they came out of the bushes, making their way down the hill under the cover of pitch darkness, they looked like an apparition of two ghosts floating toward them. A sense of dread instantly gripped the two girls, almost paralyzing them, the neighbors heard a blood curdling scream let out at the top of their lungs as they hightailed back inside the house cowering in the corner of the bedroom, shaking from head to toe. Only after hearing the laughter that followed them inside the house were they able to regain their senses.

The "Boozee back" or the "Monkey band" as it was called attracted men who would wipe dirty engine oil all over their bodies and faces and wear a diaper like loin cloth to which was attached a long tail configured with the same material tightened with a certain consistency as it trailed the wearer. They would carry a shoe box and invited the children to pay the obligatory ten cents to view the mysterious content. If anything it was their love of the element of surprise that motivated them to part with their money and pay these men to be amused by the discovery that the inside of the box contained a dead lizard, or a frog, or any small insignificant insect.

Every Carnival had to have several Monkey Bands. A monkey band consisted of a group of men playing what is called a 'bum drum.' It is a homemade steel drum strung around the shoulders of the players. The men would play different syncopated rhythms turning into a highly energetic pageantry. There were always a few men dressed up in different attires who were actually the 'dangers,' meaning, the one who scared kids, all in good fun. Franklyn, Vonley, and Russell would dress up in their mothers' clothes picked from the clothes line while they were hanging out to dry and run all around Sion Hill unconcerned whatever people might think. Then there was this other man who went by the name of "Weatherman" who devised his unique form of entertainment. He would select a three by three piece of plywood, cut out a hole large enough to fit the top of his bald head. For ten cents, each child as well as adults who would also join in the fun, got a tennis ball and used it to hit Weatherman on the head. One had to wonder how hard Weatherman's skull was for not displaying any side effect that we kids could see. It is a valued guess to believe that being under the influence of the local strong rum—120 proof—any pain to his head was quickly anesthetized.

Three long years filled with pregnant expectations had already passed since Leslie left for America in 1961. Franklyn and his brother were assured that their papers were in the works, albeit a tedious, painstakingly slow process that was not disclosed. A letter addressed to Lennox Michael Seales finally arrived with specific instructions to go to Barbados on November 23, 1964 and report to the American Consulate. Franklyn's name surprisingly was omitted and he wondered why, but the fortunate one of the two could not dispute the fact that he was next, perhaps simply by the luck of the draw. Franklyn had hoped or rather knew that he was next on line. He was, however, too preoccupied with his activities to succumb to a state of self-pity. He spent no time in morbid reflections and accepted his fate. So it was thought. The passengers were to set sail at 8:00 PM that Sunday, which kept Lennox awake the night before in anticipation of what he dreamt for many years. The excitement of taking the trip kept him from going to the beach for a swim as they usually did every Sunday, a ritual they observed from birth, he instead spent the day greeting and saying his goodbyes to friends in the village and those who stopped by the house. He found himself lost in the unknown that awaited him leaving the island, the neighborhood, the village, the people. That's all he has ever known. He felt elation and sadness all mixed in. Afternoon came and Lessie as usual wa s busy cooking his last meal that was shared with friends who lingered around. Amidst the laughter he is feeling waves of sadness assaulting his senses, hearing his friends wishing him well and bidding him farewell.

Six PM comes and uncle John Phils arrives at the house to pick him up. He gives Lessie a hug and feels her powerful arms squeezing him very tightly for a few seconds that feels longer and hear her sobbing and see tears streaming down her cheeks. "You be good now Lennox . . . don't forget me and come back to see me again . . ." He feels a sudden pressure against his throat that interrupts the flow of air, his head feels unexpectedly light, but he gasps and recover to utter words of *"thank you . . . I will come back"* to his 'mama' Lessie. It was a bitter sweet departure that affirmed the bond Lessie and Lennox had for the sixteen years of his life.

From the corner of his eyes, Lennox catches Franklyn standing at a distance seemingly lost in his thoughts. He does not look like the gregarious brother he knows. He approaches him and taps him on the shoulder. His body tenses up as if someone had pulled him from a place he did not want to be, and at the same time swivels his head toward the direction of the touch. He wears an uncharacteristically somber look on his face. He looks at his brother with eyes that seem to go through him and out of focus.

"Hey Franklyn, why did you walk away from us, what's the matter?"

"Nothing . . . really . . ." he says unconvincingly.

"Hey, everything will be alright. You will soon join us" trying to cheer him.

"But when?"

"I don't know but soon. Ma is working on your papers, you know that," pressing to cheer him up again.

"I thought we would be leaving together." Franklyn was expressing real pain and sorrow.

"I know but . . ."

"How do you think I feel"-interrupting him in mid sentence-" Leslie is gone, now you are leaving, Dad is away, Joy went to Trinidad and nobody knows if or when I will ever leave this island."

He finds himself at a loss for words. Franklyn was expressing frustration he never anticipated hearing from him. He is taken aback by this change in his demeanor that he'd never seen before. It's a guess he had reached his emotional break point we are all heir to.

"I'm sure you will hear from Ma soon. You still have Pat and Lessie to look after you." Trying to console him was not getting anywhere.

"If anybody deserves to leave now, it's me . . . why you?"

"I don't know Franklyn . . ." Lennox was stomped.

"Anyway," he hears him sigh, "I will have your bicycle by myself," he surprisingly injects. His voice rings a familiar tone that sounds like the Franklyn he knows. His eyes dart to look at him and recognize his countenance had changed with his last sentence.

"Yes, you will. You can use it anytime you want." Lennox cheerfully says.

Franklyn's face brightens up and he is once again back to his old self. Lennox feels a renewed sense of relief that life for Franklyn will go on as it always has, now that he had turned twelve but experienced life of someone twice that age. *"I wish I could take him along. I wonder how he will adjust to life without me at his side. Will he remain true to his dreams or become distracted by unknown influences?"* Lennox wonders. Only time will tell.

Pat, her kids and Franklyn accompany Lennox to town. The drive to the port is marred by an unfamiliar air of sadness. No words are exchanged during the half hour ride to the destination. As they arrive, Lennox kisses his sister in an embrace and her children, gives Franklyn a hug and whisper, *"I will write to you."* He nods approvingly. Uncle John, a close friend of the family, paid his passage on the Carib Clipper and gave him a few bucks for pocket change. He hands him an envelope containing the papers for the American Consulate, "Good bye young man," he wishes this boy.

The Carib Clipper, with a rather fancy name, was unlike other boats that were better known as "Ram Goat" vessels, so called because the boats actually transported goats from one Island to the next. They combined passengers and goats on the same voyage to Barbados, Grenada, and Trinidad. He holds on tightly to his bag as he proceeds to board the Clipper while looking for familiar faces that are making the voyage. He vaguely recognizes one or two people as he secures a seat on the deck. After a few minutes, they pull anchor, and the captain slowly navigates the vessel out of the harbor. *"I look back as we drift away from land,"* Lennox observes. *"The water is calm and the ocean breeze caresses my face. I can recognize dimmed lights in Kingstown, Montrose and Cane Garden. Soon my island is dwarfed by the expanse of empty sea surrounding us. Then suddenly a swell of emotions gallops to overtake me. I feel giddy with excitement while drops of tears flow down my cheeks at the thought that my life, from this moment on, is taking a drastic direction that could not be foretold. I resign myself to the unknown while holding to the firm belief that New York will welcome its newest immigrant. I quickly snap back into the moment and look around me, gazing at the faces of the men and women lost in their own thoughts and notice that I am the youngest passenger on board. I catch the gaze of the same man who a few minutes before looked vaguely familiar as I boarded the boat. I see him take a few steps in my direction. I quickly drop my eyes as he approaches, he leans toward me and hear him say,*

"Are you Frank Seales' son"?

I pick up my head and say, "Yes sir, I am," affirming his guess.

"I knew I recognized you. You look like your daddy . . . going to Barbados?"

"Yes sir, but I'm going to America." I'm barely able to contain my excitement.

"Hey, lucky you . . . who do you know in America son?"

Odd question I thought of him asking.

"My mother sent for me to join her and my sister." I respond with clear emphasis.

"Good for you son . . . good for you . . . good luck."

His voice trails as he walks away.

"Thank you sir . . ." I don't think he heard me.

My dad was known all around Kingstown and I felt secured in the company I met on the boat; then I heard the whimper of someone saying,

"He's going to America to meet his mama . . . I wish it was me."

The dark sky over Barbados is slowly dissipating giving way to the pale morning mist. One can see the sky and the sea mating in their colorful splendor. One stares over the horizon as the eyes gradually begin piercing the dawn of this new day to record an emerging picture of a flat mass of land growing larger as the boat nears the shores. Though Lennox has been on a boat along the Grenadines before, nothing matched the Carib Clipper and the distance traveled lasting more than twelve hours. Upon arrival on terra firma, he is greeted by Miss Joe and George who give him the impression they enjoy having him as their guest. He spends the next three days finalizing the paper work at the American consulate and taking some walks around Barbados on his first trip to a foreign land. Then, on November 27th 1964, time finally arrived to say goodbye to the hosts and head on for the airport where he boards a Pan Am flight to New York. A white American woman occupied the seat next to his and very courteously began to speak to him. He hears her mention "Thanksgiving Day," a holiday that is observed in America on the day of the flight, something he knows nothing about.

"Hi, you are going to New York . . . have you been there before?" *I hear this smiling feminine voice coming from the seat to my left.*

"No mum, this is my first trip."

"You have relatives living in New York?"

"My mother and my sister live there."

"How nice. Are you going on a vacation?"

"No mum, I am going to become a permanent resident. I left St Vincent three days ago."

"Oh, you're Vincentian. I've been to your island; it's a beautiful place, nice people. You know, New York is a big city . . ."

"I heard."

"I've lived in Barbados for the past fifteen years and love it. I'm going to NY to celebrate Thanksgiving with my relatives."

"Oh, what's Thanksgiving?" I responded quizzically.

"Oh, silly me . . . Thanksgiving is a traditional American holiday we celebrate in November of each year . . . It's the harvest festival celebrated primarily in the United States and Canada. Thanksgiving is associated with giving thanks to God for the harvest and expressing gratitude. It dates back to the early Pilgrims."

"Wow, very nice. I am very thankful for the opportunity to travel to New York on this feast day, huh?"

"Yes, you should be."

His travelling companion pushes back her seat and closes her eyes. He's too excited to fall asleep like others he notices in the cabin. Time passes. By then the captain's voice is heard on the overhead speakers: "Ladies and gentlemen, we are preparing for landing. We should be on the ground at the John F. Kennedy airport in less than ten minutes. Fasten your seatbelts. I trust you enjoyed your flight, and we thank you for choosing Pan Am."

"Wow, time has gone by very quickly," Lennox remarks. He feels the excitement growing as he looks out of the window and notices what looks like millions of bulbs glowing in the darkness. As the airplane continues to descend he's able to recognize the shape of massive buildings that dot the landscape. "What have we here!" He can barely contain his schoolboy euphoria, when his travelling companion whispers,

"I wish you well in your new life in New York young man."

"Thank you mum. I appreciate it and I wish you well also."

One feels the sudden and the hard jolt of the plane as the back tires hit the tarmac then drops parallel to the ground and continues rolling to its final designated stop. The lights in the cabin come on, and everyone gets up to retrieve their carryon luggage. One by one passengers disembark. Lennox follows the line. As soon as he exits the aircraft, a blast of icy cold air sends chills through his entire body. He attempts to take a deep breath to fill his lungs but this causes him to quickly exhale and cough violently for a brief moment. He had left the clean, fresh aromatic tropical air behind to be greeted with the pollutants that hover the landscape of the most powerful industrialized nation on earth. All passengers are directed to the Customs officers. His papers, he's told, are in order. After clearing immigration, He follows passengers ahead of him and then he is finally greeted by a strong hug by mother Olive and Carlton who hands him a heavy wool coat before leaving the heated airport. The same blast of artic air greets him as they walk to an open parking area where they board Carlton's car. They drive through streets and neighborhoods with houses built close to each other, Lennox stares in amazement. All the trees seemed to have been cut down. They proceed to a house located on Quincy street in Brooklyn where his sister Leslie and him are finally reunited.

THE VISITORS

Franklyn witnessed the Foxworth family arrival from England on a breezy April Sunday. Their plane had had difficulty landing on the tiny strip of runway, and Mrs. Foxworth was heard to mutter in her crisp, denture accent as she passed through customs, that she needed a stiff drink. Mr. Foxworth holding the hands of his daughters on each side of him for support, looked exasperated, tired and mortified that this was the place where he would have to spend perhaps years on account of his health.

They settled in a comfortable colonial home belonging to another Englishman who owned two hotels on the island, and hired two maids and a man to tend their garden. Life was made easier for Mr. Foxworth when he discovered other English residents on the island. The Foxworths quickly ingratiated themselves with them and were often guests at the Governor General home, and they settled into colonial life with less trepidation than when they first arrived.

Their lives in England had been extravagant and rowdy. Mr. Foxworth, a small man, brisk and knock-kneed always giving the appearance of a puppy that had not fully developed into a grown dog, was a talented race car driver in his youth and prime, who had competed in races in England and Europe though never with much success. His only claim to fame was his shameless sense of humor during those competitions in the late forties and early fifties, when he found himself losing, which was always the case, coming second to last place or much too often, dead last. He would rise out of his seat while steering the car and drop his trousers to reveal shorts made from the Union Jack, or for a little bit of variety, white shorts with either blue or red lettering that said 'Rule Britannia!' The Foxworth were constantly photographed for the newspapers and magazines and gave wonderful wild parties at their place on the Riviera and at their house in London. In between their jaunts, two daughters were born, but after what Mrs. Foxworth thought was the obligatory motherhood break-in period, she thrust the girls into the hands of maids and nannies and was off again with her husband.

Her father was a knight who received that honor for services as an architect and land developer in India, and his daughter had been given the best of an English gentlewoman's upbringing.

Joan Foxworth was a horse compared to her puppy-dog husband. Not that she was ugly by any means but her heightened grandeur made her into something of an awkward giraffe. No, she was a beautiful woman, and dressed to fit her lean cantilevered body in the most tasteful of clothing.

Her husband, Vivyan Foxworth, has pushed his living too hard and was found to be suffering from tuberculosis. He was sent to a sanitarium in France and then to another in Scotland, then dispatched to the island because of a weak heart that completed his frustrations, for a year or two's rest to rebuild his strength. He had objected to leaving behind the life he so enjoyed, but he was not getting any younger and the cars were different than the simple ones he rushed around in the forties. He also slowly found out that his practical jokes were worn out from overuse, and Joan thought it would be a good idea to enjoy the short spell of recuperation while giving their growing daughters the attention so sorely absent when they were younger. They threw a huge party and departed from England.

Joan was always a drinker, with Vivyan following not too hard behind. She had started early, and now with the island life boxing her in, she indulged more than ever. After an incident that took place during a party at the Governor General's house, they were dropped from the regular guest list. In a moment of uninhibited solace, Vivyan had stepped into the fountain on the grounds of the mansion and singing 'God save the king' at the top of his lungs, had dropped his pants to the embarrassed horror of the island's aristocracy and the hoi polloi. This time he had forgotten to wear his Union Jack shorts. To add to the confusion, Joan had lovingly joined Vivyan and let her panties slip into the water to join the unhappy goldfishes.

To ease what they considered a calculating pretentious affair, they had drunkenly lost footing and fell from the top rung of the Island's hierarchy. They were never asked to the Governor's again and word spread that Joan and Vivyan Foxworth had turned into hopeless drunks. The money from Vivyan's estate and from the magazine in London for which he had written some funny articles on colonial life was running low. There was still enough though, but with servants stealing their belongings while they lay drunk about their house, and the upkeep of it, they were forced to move to a smaller but still comfortable house in the Indian Bay section of the island.

The two years stretched into fourteen and the daughters of the Foxworth left the Island. The elder married an Englishman and moved with him to another island in the Caribbean and the younger went to England to attend school. Neither of them communicated much with their parents.

The Foxworths attended the Anglican Church on Sundays. They walked there since the authorities had confiscated Vivyan's license after his tenth accident that left them only shaken and cut but had instantly killed a local boy and three of his sheep which he had been grazing. Luckily for them that they happened to be brought sober before the magistrate and that stretch of road had been a noted treacherous corner. They had paid for the boy's funeral and appeased his family with a sum of money.

Carnival on the island was an occasion for festivities that lasted three days. Small in comparison with the extravaganzas in Rio, but with as much gusto and excited preparations: Days of drinking, dancing and partying. The steel bands marched through the narrow streets of Kingstown, with music punctuating the calypso-singing throngs. Colors flung themselves at the eyes and drunkened the senses even more than they were. The glitter of hundreds of headpieces worn by the carnival celebrants, dazzled and bewitched with their beauty. Many were Franklyn's creations. It was in the midst of this bacchanal that Franklyn and his posse of five dubbed the Foxworths, "Mr. and Mrs. Rumbo." After carnival ended, when everyone headed for church to have ashes swiped on their forehead on Ash Wednesday. The name was laughingly brought up to retell some story of the carnival behavior of Mr. and Mrs. Rumbo.

The Foxworths moved again, this time into a small bungalow in a new neighborhood. Their once orderly island life lavished chaotically around them. In their twenty-four hour stupor, they carried on happily, unaware of the eyes that found them sad and humiliating. When once they had been snobbish and aloof to the poorer natives, in their liquor-freeing state, they allowed themselves to be friendly with them and found new friends in them. Vivyan could often be seen having a drink in their company at a Calliaqua rum shop, attempting to sing snatches of West Indian songs when one of the partiers pulled out his four stringed 'quatro' or a beaten up guitar. There was joy on his face, smiling puppy-like and red. Soon he would collapse at the table and one of his drinking partners would help him home under the star-filled sky, or as the early sun sent its first ray of light.

Joan became more of a recluse and seldom ventured out except when sober, to walk along the beach and take a swim in the calm water of the bay. Her once dignified body was beginning to show the liquor beating, her face though was fighting back a haggardness and was thinner and more defined. Her cheekbones gave the illusion that they were higher, but that was only because her cheeks were sunken and pulled tight against the bone. With red lips painted haphazardly with a stick of bright rouge, she always had a ready smile for those she met on her walk. She still maintained a commanding air about her, but she moved sadly with the determination of an outbound sloop, its sails full of air, cutting through the green water with a deceptive power and grace.

The Foxworths in their new home made a few good friends with some of the middle class locals; drinking friends who had them over for dinner and parties. The two were often a delight to the company with their memories and philosophical anecdotes. They seemed to be understood by those they now counted as their friends while Vivyan accepted a local job at the island's Tourism Center with an office overlooking the bay where the ships entered. Their lives took on a new phase in this community of friends and Joan drank less, making Vivyan copy her. They opened up their bungalow to guests for dinners and afternoon parties and hired a new maid to help them keep up with the local gossip. Their daughters communicated with them more often now and in the midst of this sunlit environment that surrounded them, they glowed with a special rebirth and satisfaction. They could always be seen at local cricket matches, Joan in a straw hat with a hibiscus flower stuck in its rim and Vivyan flaunting himself in a colorful sport shirt cheering on their team. Sometimes sitting regally on their veranda on their white wicker chairs, they would watch the tide come in to cover the pink and white coral on the reef, shadows of the myriad colors tinting the blue water for a moment. The anchored boats in the bay turned and pulled on their anchor chains with the wind and above them in the trees humming birds glistened by collecting water drops and syrup from the flowers. Naked children ran laughing on the beach daring the warm water to catch them as the evening waves lapped the shoreline comforting them and making them at last feel themselves a part of this startling painting of nature.

They had always been very much in love and in this reverie they realized this even more. Vivyan became Vivies and Joan was called Punch after the drink she loved so much. They made Sundays their drinking day and were often drunk before they arrived at the church door for the service. Sometimes Joan would kneel for a moment of prayer and remain in that position for the rest of the service. Those seated further away thought this gesture of humility to be a very admirably pious act. Those closer heard her tranquil snores as the priest continued with his homily.

The Foxworths never moved again from their home. The maid left after a year, and their lives plunged once more into one of the unplanned nonchalance. The Sunday drinking became weekly binges. Vivyan swam out into the ocean one day and promptly sank. He was rescued by a friend. As they grew older, they helped accelerate the aging process by defying it in every sense. The friends dropped away from them suddenly like a quick tide. They were called nuisances and the poorer locals looked down at them as Mr. and Mrs. Rumbo staggered down the countryside road walking to nowhere in particular. The oldest daughter and her husband arrived unexpectedly and took them away on a short vacation, but not many days later to the surprise of no one, they returned to pick up where they left off.

Disembarking from the small Liat plane that brought them back home, Joan fell down the steps onto the runway and broke her left leg, and Vivyan was said to have laughed out loud and called her a clumsy cow. Her walk was never the same after the leg healed; she took less care in her appearance. Her lustrous head of hair was brushed flat against her skull, her lipstick, a margin of error as it zigzagged from lips to chin, she smoked heavily and her clear speech was always slurred.

Vivyan continued his job, but only out of sympathy for his superior. Their house turned into a mess that their lives had patterned. They ate out of half-opened cans, consequently suffering from bouts of food poisoning, and Vivyan was hospitalized for his heart condition. They did not allow themselves to be seen on their veranda anymore, but stayed indoors and read or screamed at each other impatiently. One Sunday the priest stopped the service and asked them to leave the church before he continued. They had been arguing about who should hold the hymnal. Vivyan, angry at being asked to leave, once more dropped his trousers in defiance and was promptly escorted out of the building by the ushers, his thin voice singing "Praise God from whom all blessings flow."

Mr. and Mrs. Rumbo kept indoors and were rarely seen. Joan developed a bad cough that persisted, and their fights could be heard in the area by those who lived closest. One night Joan found Vivyan slumped over; his hand had ripped down the shower curtain in an effort to steady himself. She did not call for help from her former friends or the police. She called her daughter who flew in from the other island the next day. Her mother had dressed Vivyan and laid him on the bed. His body was flown back to England to be buried. Joan did not take the trip. She remained at her daughter's house till the end of her life.

*   *   *

Franklyn 10 years old

Dear Mum,

This is me. I took out this picture up at the rectory by the priest; his aunt has just arrived from America. The sun was behind my head that is why it turn white. Mum he is very kind to me. When I had my cold since Lessie left he gave me honey mixture and it did me very well. All the kids are well also. Debbie is well too she love her dolly she takes her to church but she wants some other dresses.

your dear son, Franklyn

Franklyn, at ten years of age, sent this picture to our mother with a tender note written in the back. We know the old cliché that a picture is worth a thousand words, so here we see a very happy Franklyn showing no outward sign of separation from his parents. This was the quintessential Franklyn, always keeping an optimistic attitude regardless of the challenges he encountered. As the older brother, I should have been the one leading the charge, but he was obviously the one to be emulated. Two years had already passed since I last saw Franklyn and in spite of the letters he wrote, I had to resign myself that the day of our reunion was anyone's guess.

The year 1967 came bringing excitement mixed with disillusionment. Pat's letter to report to the American embassy arrived just like it did for Lennox and Leslie. Franklyn was once again thrown into a state of bewilderment that was very hard to take let alone understand that he was by all indications almost abandoned by the family. Their father who was working in Trinidad returned to St Vincent when he heard of Pat's pending departure and to reunite with his youngest for a few days. A call came from his mother to speak with Franklyn who had questions he needed answered: "How long should I wait to leave for America, Ma?" Franklyn's question was unequivocal. She explained to Franklyn that it was best to finish his schooling and in another year his papers should be completed for his departure. In fact, she said, "papers were filed for both you and your father to migrate to the US at the same time."

"Are you sure Ma?" Franklyn queried.

"Yes son, I'm sure, all will be fine in another year. I promise."

"Ma, I've waited and waited and when the letter came I was sure I was going to leave after Michael. It's been three years since he left, Ma," Franklyn said plaintively. "I don't understand why I have to be the last one to leave, Ma . . . everybody's gone."

"I know son. It won't be long . . ." Ma's voice was trembling.

"Okay Ma, write soon."

"Yes Franklyn, I'll write soon."

"As she clicks off, Ma burst into tears burying her face in her hands," Lennox recounts. *"She then slowly turns and raises her eyes to me; her eyelashes matted with tears, seeking a word of comfort, I hear her plaintive voice say, 'What can I do?' but I remain mute. I cannot find the words she is seeking. At that moment, I feel totally inadequate, walk backward through the open door, putting distance between us without responding. I leave her alone in the room to gather her thoughts."*

How long will it take for a letter from America to reach Calliaqua was not a rhetorical question for a young man with his dreams. Franklyn had it all visualized and mapped out very concretely, consumed with the idea that he would one day go to an America that would offer every opportunity to apply his God-given talents, for his dreams to materialize and become famous in an industry that no Vincentian of his generation or past has ever claimed.

Life for Franklyn continued without missing a beat. He followed his script to the letter, spending much of his time at the Minors with his friend, Antoinette, who acted as a younger sister. He would also stay at the Phils' house instead of returning to Calliaqua spending many days and nights in their company. Parcels of clothing were coming and letters from America with money were delivered to help him while away the days. Steph lived in Calliaqua with her children who were Franklyn's siblings. He had a particular fondness for his sister, Jennifer, who like Antoinette enjoyed his company. He practically took control of their lives advising them what to wear, how to conduct themselves in public, who they should choose for friends, what books to read. A classmate of his, Murray, was deemed suitable for Franklyn to choose him as a boyfriend for his sister Jennifer.

THE GANG OF SIX
AND THE FISHERMAN

Leslie Dougan was beginning to hate his first name with a strong passion that troubled his friends. Why did his parents choose that name that could easily be mistaken for a girl's? He was fast approaching his twelfth birthday which fell on an August day during the summer vacation. Ever since he had allowed his three visiting girl cousins to dress him up in one of their frocks, paint his lips and eyes and play 'beauty contest' and word got back to the five friends he usually played with, he had detected a contemptuous look in their eyes as if they were on the verge of exploding into uncontrollable sardonic laughter.

Velma, the group's girl leader and best swimmer, grabbed his khaki shorts one day and pulled them down to his knees to see if he "had one." Her mouth puckered and giggles squeezed out when she saw that he did. After composing herself, she said, "Is this the way they look, all shriveled up? I'm glad I don't have one." The other four friends nodded their heads in agreement like doctors diagnosing a bedridden patient. Mary, the other girl, who Leslie thought liked him more than the others, covered her eyes and the hair-scalp spaces between the rows of parted plaits on her head, went crimson. She did not remove her hands from her face until Leslie had ample time to pull his shorts back up to his navel and stuff his shirt tail into them.

Mary was kind and gentle most of the time, except when someone pulled on her long plaits or she happened upon a sand crab. When she saw one of the fidgety creatures crisscrossing sideways on the smooth beach ahead of her, her round cherubic face would crease into a waxy glazed look, and grabbing the nearest rock, she would hurl it with every ounce of power at the unsuspecting animal, usually smashing its shell hard back with an accuracy that amazed everyone. Leslie admired her even more, and thought that she might even love him. One day she had scrawled his name on the sand and put hers under it, encircling them with a big heart. From that moment on, Leslie was completely devoted to Mary, even to the point of walking ahead of her on the beach to chase away any crab that might upset her stroll.

Franklyn, the artist in the group, was respected even more with the arrival on the Island of a ballpoint pen that could write in blue and red, just by snapping one of the little plastic pegs on its tip. He was a master at creating butterflies. He would sit before a white sheet of copy book paper and in no time at all, have the most beautiful red and blue insects on the page. He also had the unforgiving distinction of having gotten sick after succumbing to a dare and drinking rum to prove he was as strong as the rest of them, then throwing up all over the altar of the church where he served as the altar boy. Father Michael had met with him, sat him down in his office:

"What's going on with you Franklyn . . . this is the second time this has happened?"

"I don't know father."

"Someone told me they saw you drinking rum. Is this true?"

"What . . . who . . . me? No."

"Don't lie to me young man . . . don't you lie to me!!! You were never a problem before. What's going on? Could it be you're missing your mother and father?" I can understand that.

"I don't know . . . maybe."

"I know it must be hard on you. I want you to come to me and talk about it, and I don't want to ever . . . I say, never want to hear someone saying they saw you drinking. Is that understood?"

"Yes sir."

"Hold it. I changed my mind. I want to see you in my office every Monday and Friday after you've done your school work. Is that understood? I want you to report to me because in the absence of your parents, I want to know what you are doing . . . you can go now."

"But . . . why every Monday and Friday?"

"Don't you ask me why . . . you hear me?"

"Yes Pastor."

Village people denounced him and said he was no good, and the sooner his mother who had migrated to America sent for him the better. He was also caught drawing naked women with breasts and men with penises in his Arithmetic copy book. The headmaster of his school had flogged him with the cowhide leather strap placed on his desk, and asked him if he had ever seen a woman's breast. He had replied, "I always saw my older sisters' because we sometimes take showers together so Lessie can scrub us down." The headmaster gave him three more stinging lashes with the thick strap and told him that in the future, he must draw people with their clothes on and sent him back to his class with a note for his teacher. Before stepping away, Franklyn said contemptuously,

"What was that for?"
"You want some more young man . . . now go . . . out of my office!!!"

Franklyn finally turned around putting space between himself and that cowhide leather strap while muttering unintelligible words he hoped the headmaster did not hear.

Barney was the strongest of the mixed-blood group, and the poorest. His mother did the washing for families around the area. He was the boy leader and the best fighter in the group. Whenever they decided to wage war with the group from the other bay, Barney was always on the front lines, acquiring the worst injuries of the group during the attacks. For each battle, Mary walked with a little bottle of iodine and some cotton balls from her mother's medicine chest to dab on the cuts and scrapes of the fighters. Barney had a deep contagious laugh that made the others feel inadequate, so they tried to copy it without much success. When Vilma that day had exposed

Leslie before the group, it was Barney who had collapsed on the ground and laughed the loudest, proudly wetting his dirty shorts in the process.

The fifth friend Anthony, who everyone called "Shaggy" ever since he had attempted to boil his cocker spaniel Shaggy in a large pot, had a face filled with freckles and a persistently runny nose. His mother worked at the telephone exchange in town, and read English love novels as she put calls through at the switchboard. When Shaggy was laid up in bed with a bout of bronchitis, which was most of the time, he had the feeling that the only illness anyone in the world could have was bronchitis. When he attended a funeral with his mother, he always imagined the departed had died from bronchitis. When he was not in bed with an attack though, he was an asset to the battles because he was the only one who could successfully tackle and overcome the tougher girls from the other bay. Barney had refused to fight them anymore after one skirmish where he had returned glistening from Mary's iodine that covered the finger nail scratch wounds of two particular opponents. Shaggy though, had returned a kind of hero for he had rescued Barney with a technique he perfected to handle the girls. Pinning their arms behind their backs with one arm, he would use the other to blow a full nose of watery snot into their hair, making them run off squealing in disgust.

Standing before his friends in dismay, Leslie appeared calm; but he bit into his lower lip as he adjusted his shorts. He looked at Barney writhing on the ground and almost laughed along with him, but he was angry and would not let himself laugh this time. He wanted to hit

Velma hard in the mouth, the way he had seen his cook's husband do, making her lips swell and bleed. He only clinched his fists at his side, and tried not to let the tears come. He swallowed many times and concentrated hard on being angry so he would not open up and just bawl. He now believed even more that they all remained his friends because his father owned a boat anchored in the bay and on which he took them all on sailing trips round the island.

School was on summer vacation and the six friends were having another hard day deciding what to do. They recently had a war, so another one was out of the question for another two weeks or so. Leslie breathed easier when it was turned down. He always became ill as soon as they made preparations for war, during and after it. The last excursion into enemy territory led by Barney had left them swollen for a few days from the bee stings that plastered their faces. Barney found a bee hive high in a tamarind tree, in the mountains and the six of them tried to collect honey from the angry bees using only old sheer stockings Mary and Leslie had collected from their mothers. Their parents were furious when they returned from their mountain escapade, their eyes almost shut tight, their cheeks puffy from the numerous stings. They were prevented from seeing each other for a week and a half, so now that they were back together, they had to be more careful about the games or adventures they undertook.

They decided not to go to Mary's house to play snakes and ladders, since her mother inevitably pulled out books they had read many times before, or played them a scratchy recording of 'Peter and the Wolf' on the phonograph. Her mother always insisted on playing with them too, and this made them feel uncomfortable as Mary lapsed into a sudden silence. Her mother had been to the asylum twice, but she always fed them well. They loved the cookies and soda she gave them, but the prospect of having to read those books, listen to a scratchy entrance of the hunters one more time and play snakes and ladders with Mary's mother, did not appeal to them in the least. Barney's ideas were out of the question. They were not even supposed to be seen with him since their parents said that "Barney created mischief, his mother was low class and he had a foul mouth."

Velma wanted to swim and play a game of hide and go seek in the water, a special game she had invented. The hiders would swim out into the water where it was deep, and the seekers would swim after them to try and tag them on the head. The only chance of getting back to shore was to sink into the depths below you and swim underwater below the catcher to scramble up onto the beach to safety.

It was too early in the day to swim though, since once you did you had to go home to rinse off the salty water. The parents seeing you, always kept you in to study, and that would be a totally wasted day. They agreed however to swim later on the day, but until then, something must be found to make the hours go faster.

"Let's collect shells and make animals to sell to tourists." Mary suggested.

"We did that last week" Shaggy sniveled, "besides, there isn't any glue or pipe cleaners left."

They had used the discarded pipe cleaners from Mary's father to support the neck section of some of the more unwieldy animals.

"How about a big sand trap?" grinned Shaggy.

Another game was digging a deep hole in the sand, covering it with thin sticks ripped out of the coconut tree fronds lying on the beach, then some leaves and more sand to make it look like just another spot of beach. When some innocent person strolled by, one leg would fall through into the hole half-filled with water.

"We'll most likely bump into crabs," said Mary "and if we dig a very big hole we'll get dirty, and that means going home to wash."

Franklyn always suggested they draw pictures in the sand, and he was always turned down since his figures were much better than the others' spindle-like executions. Leslie had no suggestions and because he was still upset, he kept quiet on purpose in the hope that the others would ask him for one. He was very worried about the situation with his name, and his stomach felt stuffed as if he had just eaten a big meal. He had always been worried about his value to the group and with this new turn of events, he felt a desperate need to do or say something clever to be on their good side again.

He hated going to war, but always marched along with them on the appointed day, and was especially grateful that Barney would assign him the puniest soldier of the enemy. But after he had overcome the frightened boy by removing his thick spectacles, marked a 'P' for prisoner on his forehead with a black crayon and sat down with his grateful prisoner to watch the rest of the battle, he always felt ashamed and hopeless. Even Mary was fighting. Her legs dealing ferocious kicks to anyone in her way. With her eyes shut tight during the battle, she more than once dealt more blows to her own side than the enemy, but she always finished the war. Leslie was afraid of losing her along with the others. His brain was working harder than it ever did to come up with something to do, but all he could think about was his name. He hated it so much, he couldn't think about anything else at the moment.

They wandered the long beach back and forth that afternoon. They walked on patches of reefs left exposed by the tide and poked at sea anemones and spiny urchins, cracking open the latter to watch the yellow jelly inside ooze out and washed by the waves. The bright sun and clear sky went unnoticed by the bored group, their eyes attacking anything of interest to spur them onto a game to alleviate their restlessness. Barney climbed a tall coconut tree at one point but couldn't make the top. He slid down quickly, ripping his pants to add yet another hole for his mother to patch. They were beginning to throw sand balls at one another when Leslie piped up,

"My father is selling his boat . . ."

The group suddenly dropped their weapons and stared at him in disbelief,

". . . but he's getting a new, better, bigger one from Trinidad," he quickly assured them.

"When is it coming?" asked Franklyn. In all honesty, he had gotten tired of seeing the same boat anchored in the same place, with the same blue color, with the same streak of white down the side.

"Soon" said Leslie smiling at him,

"We'll all get to go on it soon."

"Will it be faster than the old one?" inquired Velma while making a wet sand ball.

"It has a better engine than the 'Sea Fly'" Leslie said, pointing at the boat in the harbor.

"Maybe we'll get to go down the islands, instead of just circling this one." Franklyn, drawing another face in the sand with his finger, resignedly opined,

"I'm so tired of this damn island."

"Our island is one of the most beautiful in the West Indies," Leslie said abruptly and wished he hadn't. He didn't want them to concentrate on such ideas, knowing full well that his father did not like to leave the island's shoreline when he sailed. Well, it wasn't his father, but his mother. She got dreadfully sick when she couldn't see any land, and Leslie was almost positive that his mother would not allow his father to change their regular route.

"I know it's a beautiful island Leslieeeee."

The annoying tone registered in Franklyn's voice again and Leslie winced and wished that someone would throw a sand bomb at him. The others had noticed the change in Franklyn's voice when he said Leslie's name and they looked at each other and smiled. "But . . ." Franklyn was going on and Leslie held his breath as if to stop him from saying his name again. He didn't.

"Even though it's beautiful, I'm tired of seeing it. I want to see other places and people. Maybe we could go to England or you could drop me off in America to see my mother! Did you say it was a big boat? It gets rough out there near America."

"Yes, it's big" Leslie almost whispered, grateful that he didn't say his name in that nasty tone again.

"What a great time we could have!" exclaimed Franklyn, and the others agreed noisily, their sparkling eyes betraying their own secret desires and dreams. Velma wanted to go to the tower of London and fly back home on a jet plane. She had never flown on one. Barney wanted to shake the Queen's hand, but Shaggy laughed at him saying that "the queen never shook hands with dirty, low class people." Barney said, "I would buy pretty clothes and wash myself." But, "the Queen never shook the hand of snotty nosed people either, especially those who blew it into people's heads." They argued and dragged through the slow afternoon in this way, finding nothing particularly interesting to do. The sun passed by its mid-day mark and headed West to depart in a myriad of colors to begin another night. They entered the water for the last game of the day: Velma's water hide and go seek. The water was warm at this time of day, exciting the six, boisterously twisting and twirling in it. The game felt better than before because of the kind of day it had been. They threw themselves into it with vigorous fervor. It was Velma's turn to be the catcher when she looked up the beach and saw walking towards them in the distance, Lucas, the old fisherman with his bamboo baskets and his nets thrown over his shoulders.

They had appeared on the scene with blustery talk and bravado, dismissing him as weak and spineless.

Lucas was the known village drunk. With his pock-marked face: cracked, creased and paper rough from his years on the sea and topped by a scraggly patch of mustache and beard, the gamesters were always reminded of the pictures of pirates in Mary's books or the movies. Lucas' red eyes never looked anyone in the face and his wild, matted hair was kept in rein with a piece of red flowered material which he tied around it into a knot at the back of his head. His body was large and lumbering, and he had a gruff hoarse voice. Because he would go directly to a local bar after his way home; his huff and puff voice modulated to the pace of his step.

They were terribly afraid of Lucas and would dash into the water at the first glance of him, swimming a little way from the shore. Because of their terrible fear of this man, they would start a sudden chant of harsh name calling and squealing like a pack of dogs at an intruder. There was a story that persisted, that although Lucas had spent many years out at sea, he couldn't swim. That if his boat capsized in a squall, he would be lost to the treacherous sea. No one had ever seen him in the ocean, but he was an expert sailor and fisherman. He caught more fish than any of the other fishermen who ventured out for the day.

The children stopped playing and swam in closer to Velma and Barney as the man made his way down the quiet beach. They jumped up and down excitedly at the sight of the head-bent Lucas, his low hollow singing carrying above the sound of the breaking waves to reach their ears. Their day would be complete with a good name calling of the drunken Lucas. As he got closer, the six voices echoed at him, their titillated voices combining fear and a tingling awe of the man.

"Rotten-gut Lucas!!! (a rotten-gut is used to describe someone whose fart stinks to high heaven. Very insulting on these islands)" screamed Barney almost losing his balance in the water. The others clapped the surface of the water with the palms of their hands, the white foam collecting around them.

"Stop singing you jack-ass . . . you'll scare the birds!!!" Velma shouted, topping Barney. This only urged them on more, trying to out-do and out-joke each other. They got louder and more daring as Lucas passed by humming now, his eyes staring at the sand in front of him. Leslie did not call out many names, and if he did, he did not hear them. This was another game that made him ill and his stomach feel full. He laughed tightly, and his throat hurt.

Lucas stopped in his tracks suddenly. He turned and looked at the children, his red eyes squinting to bring them into focus. He had never bothered with them before, never bothered to look at them. But there he stood today staring straight at them, standing silently now, watching them watch him. The noise in the water lessened as Lucas dropped his nets from his shoulders and put his basket of fish next to them on the sand. He reached into it and removed a narrow, sharp-pointed cutlass knife, the kind the local fishermen gutted their catch with before selling it. Velma let out a blood-curdling yell and dashed for the shore, but as Lucas hobbled towards her, she changed direction using as much energy to get back into the water beside her friends, transfixed like poles in the water.

"Swim out into the deep!!!" the cry went up. Velma, leading the way through the dazed faces. Bodies collapsed into the water and followed Velma quickly. They swam to where their feet couldn't feel the bottom anymore, and turned to face the shore watching and waiting for Lucas to retreat, but he didn't. Instead, he was slowly wading out to where they were floating comfortably, the knife gripped between his teeth. The children still waited for him to go back, he would not dare swim out into the deep and drown. To their horror, Lucas began to swim out into the deep with strong, determined strokes, his ragged cigarette-stained beard dragging in the water, the blade in his mouth.

"Dive down! Dive under him!" Mary cried out.
"Dive down!" Velma ordered.

Her head disappeared below the surface and the others followed. She led them underwater past Lucas looming above, their arms frantically pushing back the streams of what felt like leaden water, their lungs bursting from fright and no air.

Velma, Barney, Franklyn, Mary and Shaggy, scrambled onto the beach, sputtering, their legs weak and chests aching. Leslie was still in the water. He hadn't moved and the five on the beach watched terrified as Lucas got nearer to him.

Leslie felt a hot stream of water drifting out from his trunks against his legs. His heart pounded out in the water, he couldn't move. He saw the others on the beach running back and forth wildly screaming orders at him. He just saw their open mouths after a while, no sound. He refused to hear them now. He decided not to move. He would stay and let the approaching Lucas get him. In Leslie's mind, he saw the others collecting his severed head to take for his mother. She would scream and scream when they laid it down in front of her. His father would hold her close and cry a little. He would show them that he could let Lucas cut off his head and let it float in the water, when they could only play Velma's silly water game and run away in fright. He saw his severed head again, grisly and hacked off submerged in a pool of blood, its eyes opened in the late afternoon's green water. Then he saw his father's new boat. He wanted to sail in her, to run away in it, leave his mother behind and go to England and America like the others wanted, see the Tower of London. "The Tower of London?" he thought. "No, I don't want my head cut off. I want to sail away on the new boat with the others." He dove down suddenly, but it was too late. Lucas had grabbed him by the tufts of his hair. Leslie could hear his loud panting breath mixed with his own pounding heart. He could smell the strong scent of liquor on his wet face, the same scent his father had when he leaned close to him sometimes. He was going to throw up, and there was a pain in the middle of his forehead. He began to cry, but he couldn't. The others were standing on the beach, watching, frantic with fear. He could hear Mary crying. He wouldn't cry; he bit his lip, and the anger rushed. His breathing was raspy and deep. Balling up his palm into a fist, he sent it smashing into Lucas's nose. Lucas snarled and the knife fell into the water. Leslie sent his fist at Lucas' face again, this time catching him on the mouth. Lucas growled and sent a vulgar cacophony of dirty words and liquor breath at Leslie. The teeth, or the few that were left, hurt Leslie's knuckles and now the pain in his head got worse from not crying. He released the blocked sound from his throat and suddenly he was screaming at the top of his lungs:

> *"YOU JUST CUT OFF MY HEAD YOU ROTTEN-GUT!!! MY FATHER WILL HAVE THE POLICE `ON YOU. YOU JUST TRY TO CUT OFF MY HEAD YOU JACK-ASS, AND MY FATHER WILL SET THE POLICE ON YOU!!!"*

A tiny stream of blood wound its way down Lucas' wet beard as he looked at the boy quietly with an air of resignation. He just swam in one spot, next to the sobbing Leslie. When he finally got to a shallow part and his feet touched the bottom, he felt as though they were asleep. The pain in his head was gone, but now he felt faint. He walked up on the sand, his friends surrounding him as he walked by to pick up his clothes lying on the sand.

"He can swim" Leslie said whimpering. He shook violently as he distanced himself from the scene of his horrific encounter. He put on his shirt and buttoned up the front. Tears ran down his face to mingle with the water dripping from his hair. He walked up the beach to his home. The others followed behind him silently while Lucas stood in the shallow water watching the six drift further away from the scene of their encounter.

*   *   *

Franklyn had grown somewhat weary of this letter from America that would bring the news for his departure from home to the land of his dreams. He was ashamed of his temporary lapse of concentration that led him to invite his neighbor's criticisms for his uncharacteristic reprehensible behavior. He had told father Michael how sorry he was and had promised that it would never happen again. He had let it known to his five mischievous friends that he was no longer interested in getting into fights or pursuing activities unbecoming of his aspirations.

"It is time for us to grow up" he had said with an air of exasperation.

"Really?" said Velma, dubious of his friend's true motives.

"You found something better to do, Franklyn?" The derisive tone of Velma's question further irritated Franklyn.

"Look, I don't think we should waste our time any longer. There are better things we should do."

"Like what?"

"I don't know. I only know that I have better things to do."

"I know what it is with you, Franklyn. You think you're better than us now, huh? We see you hanging out in Villa and the other people in Indian Bay. That's it, right?"

"No, that's not it. We still can have some fun together, but doing the same things over and over, I get bored . . . that's all it is."

"I know you'll be going to America and you think you're better than us . . ."

"That's not it . . ."

"Yeah, that's it . . . don't tell me that's not it . . . I know you . . . pull yourself together and come back to us when you're ready."

"No I won't"

"What do you mean, you won't . . . Who do you think you're fooling?"

"Time for me to move on, that's all."

"Ok, suit yourself, Franklyn." Velma walks away shaking her head, then stops, turns to Franklyn and yells,

"Go to hell Franklyn. I don't want to play with you anymore."

Franklyn breathed a sigh of relief that he was able to get this off his chest, knowing full well the news would reach the others. This was a decision he was convinced he had to make.

Nearly a year had passed and the people at the church took notice of Franklyn's change in demeanor and had forgiven him. When the letter had finally arrived, the feeling of abandonment had festered long enough, substituted for the day he had waited for so long that had now ensnared him in an embrace that filled him with sheer ecstasy. His father had arrived from Trinidad to make final arrangements for their departure. The nanny Lessie was entering an entirely new and very difficult phase of her life that none could begin to fully understand. They meant so much to her but only time would tell.

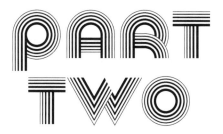

PART
TWO

Mother Olive

Lessie

10 yr. old Franklin

Leslie and Natasha

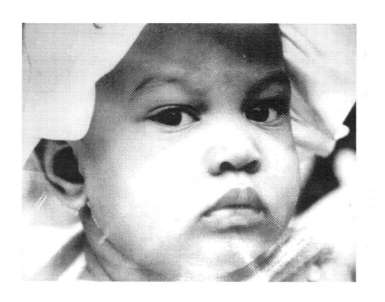

Natasha

1973–1974 Season

THE JUILLIARD SCHOOL

Peter Mennin, President

Bachelor of Fine Arts Degree

ROBERT FRANCIS BACIGALUPI, *Drama*
CHRISTINE JANE BARANSKI, *Drama*
ROBERT MAITLAND BESEDA, *Drama*
DARYL BRATCHES, *Dance*
DAVID GLENN BRIGGS, *Dance*
TIINA CATHERINE JEAN CARTMELL, *Drama*
JAN RENEE DEVEREAUX, *Drama*
JENNIFER DOUGLAS, *Dance*

VIVIAN FACUSSE, *Drama*
MARY LOUISE FAGER, *Dance*
SANDRA SARA HALPERN, *Drama*
JANE LOWE, *Dance**
NANCY RUBEL MAPOTHER, *Dance*
PAUL PANFIGLIO, *Drama*
FRANKLYN SEALES, *Drama*
PETER DAVID SPARLING, *Dance**

Out of the pool

Blowing a tune

Steph and Francis Seales

Franklyn in Italy

138

COMING TO AMERICA

July 8, 1968, at approximately 9:00 PM Eastern Standard Time, a Pam American plane lands at JFK international airport. On board is Franklyn Vincent Ellison Seales, accompanied by his father to join on American soil, mother Olive, Leslie, Pat and Lennox who had the good fortune of making it to the New World before he did. He came also to join the youngest brother Regis, born in America. In 1965 Leslie and I had married following a fortuitous meeting at a NYU college dance sponsored by the West Indian Students Association. We were present at the airport with our eleven month old daughter, Natasha, to greet the newest Seales immigrants to the "Promised Land.". Franklyn had arrived at the peak of his teenage years. His deep tan complexion could not hide the sun damage to his skin. He exhibited a certain joyfulness that was anticipated. He swept his niece from the floor whose hand Leslie was holding and planted a big kiss on each cheek as she encircled his neck with both of her tiny arms. This eleven-month-old child felt secure in her uncle's arms. I then turned my attention to Francis Adolphus Seales, the patriarch of the Seales family, my father-in-law. He was dressed in casual clothes to combat the hot, muggy New York weather. He pulled out a handkerchief from his back pocket to wipe the wetness on his forehead and brow then extended his hand that

I grabbed while silently expressing my thanks for the gift of his daughter and mother of our daughter. My father-in-law and I finally met face to face on that warm July summer night, as fate decreed it. Three years before I had written him a letter asking for the hands of his beloved daughter, Leslie. His letter of approval followed shortly.

"How are you sir, nice meeting you . . . ?" I heard my voice greeting him with an appreciative smile.

"Nice meeting you, too."

"How was your trip?"

"A little tired now, but glad to be here," A smile accompanied my father-in-law's remark.

"Let's go for your luggage."

I followed him with Franklyn still carrying our daughter in his arms and not letting go, engaging her in a conversation that she seemed to be enjoying.

To West Indians growing up in the developing world, America's streets could well be paved with gold: *Every child had access to decent schools . . . everyone worked . . . all families lived in houses with white picket fences.* After all, this was the story told in American magazines we had access to and the movies that were shown further accentuated the wonderful American way of life. One could well say we nurtured a certain naiveté. Franklyn, however, thought outside the box. He was a dreamer whose destiny he would control and prove to his contemporaries that all things are possible even for a boy who spent his childhood sharing a bed with his other siblings and rose above his circumstances. He never felt deprived and made the best of everything he had.

The Seales family occupied the upper floor of a two-family brick house located at 1661 Carroll Street. Stores of every variety lined both sides of the street, a hub of activity, which lead to the intersection many refer to as the "heart of Brooklyn," West Indian country, Eastern Parkway and Utica Ave. Franklyn had enrolled as a Junior at Abraham Lincoln High located thirty minutes away by train, where his assimilation of the American culture was surprisingly seamless. He grew his hair out sporting a huge afro-type hairstyle, very common in those days. As Franklyn moved more and more into his new environment, he showed a hunger to integrate much of his experiences to become an American. He was definitely on the fast track. He observed the lifestyle around him and took advantage of every available resource. He was given a Navy blue coat, new gloves and boots. On the home front, he began to manipulate all of the avenues opened to him in his pursuits. He was eating differently. He wanted less West Indian type foods and was more selective of the foods that he ate. His mother may have been living in America, but her heart and soul were still in the Caribbean. By contrast, Franklyn had left the Islands and was moving into the fabric of his new society, foot by foot and soon by leaps and bounds. He was going through cellular changes in our estimation. His poor mother had no clue. She began at times to see him as ungrateful given her sacrifices. We saw it as Franklyn's descent into the bosom of the America that he craved from early childhood. Mother Olive was old school West

Indian who had very little need to assimilate. She had a path that allowed her to serve her family. She found herself in her element and felt content. She was not going out of her way to join anything or anyone. Franklyn, on the other hand, sought to deny his roots at this particular juncture and focus more on the things that would bring him into the dream of being and living in the States. It was a cultural social dilemma. He would become frustrated by the West Indian flavor in the home. Franklyn would have heated exchanges with his mother, often shouting the worst insults about herself and the family. Lennox would at times eavesdrop on these conversations, recognizing the heightened level of frustration while cognizant of his mother's limitations. It was an extremely disturbing adjustment. He was witnessing Franklyn's heights of frustration and self-centered fear. He would repeat his idle threats about wanting to get away from the family and the culture. Parenthetically, his was not a unique reaction to this new world. Sidney Poitier, the renown Oscar-winning actor, in his book, "This Life," recounts with great detail his own struggles adjusting to his new environment after leaving the Bahamas for America and discovering the world of acting. Like Franklyn, he came from humble beginnings. He spoke of his rejections and determination of shedding his noticeable Bahamian accent after an encounter with the American actor, theater producer, and television director, Frederick O'Neal who founded the American Negro Theater. During an audition, Mr. O'Neal interrupted Mr. Poitier with biting criticism of his accent: *"You can hardly talk . . . you've got an accent . . . you can't be an actor with an accent like that . . . and you can hardly read . . . you can't be an actor and not be able to read."* Like a Samurai sword, the words sliced through deep and might have put an end to Sidney Poitier's aspiration of becoming an actor had it not been for his innate drive and determination that made him quickly realize that he had to *". . . take my life into my own hands and work it into something worthwhile . . . I have to find a way to prove that man wrong."*

Mr. Poitier speaks of spending hours and hours listening to radio broadcasts and repeating lines, word for word, spoken by the announcer determined to acquire the American accent. Franklyn who had never heard of Mr. Poitier was undergoing an almost similar culture shock; feelings of embarrassment and humility, a mind full of confusion and anxiety that were not part of his core makeup.

"You guys have no ambition . . . you guys are too limited and content to do and have nothing." would spit out of Franklyn's mouth, having to come to terms with what he saw as limitations.

"I can't wait to get away . . ." treating his mother with loathing and indifference.

"Finally, one night," Lennox recounts, *"after hearing him tear into Ma and witnessing the pain caused by his choice of words tantamount to psychological abuse, I felt a painful sense of outrage boiling to the surface. I paced the floor while absorbing the crucial blows administered to Ma by her son. I had heard enough and reached my breaking point. I had to do something: I walked into the kitchen, fetched a bucket of ice cold water, walked back into the living*

room finding him giving me his back still hurling his insults, and in a moment of righteous indignation, I let him have it. The water went splashing on the furniture, the curtain. He stood literally transfixed in a puddle formed where he stood, his face registering the shock of the cold water dripping from his head, down to his clothes and onto the floor, momentarily unable to utter a word. Now, up until this time, Franklyn was known to be suffering from asthma with none of the old time remedies bringing any relief. It was not long after the cold water Baptism I inflicted on him that he shared with me that his asthma had instantaneously disappeared. So it did. That night. We laughed and made light of this episode. In addition, Ma and I made certain concessions to Franklyn, not knowing all that was happening in his head, we wanted to accommodate this young man. I was already in college and working. I spent time away from the house on Carroll street as well. It helped me, and it gave Franklyn space for himself.”

Yes, there were financial limitations and also certain lacks for their participation in the master culture; however, Franklyn was seeing and realizing more of the mainstream culture than ever before. He ventured outside of himself and in his mind was not seeing it reflected in the home. There was incongruence, and it was huge. His mother was alienated and Franklyn felt a more acute sense of the estrangement. Neither could articulate fully their internal experience. Lennox, on the other hand, was the objective outsider brother who had the insight and the understanding, but Franklyn saw him as part of the problem rather than the "Mr. Fixit" role he attempted to play. His high level of frustration remained until after high school and gaining admittance to Juilliard. He was turning a new chapter in his life and becoming more the person he imagined from childhood. He was becoming the man he always wanted to be, hence finally discovering congruence in his life **vis**-à-**vis** the outside world.

Like many American families, the Seales family had one TV in the living room for their enjoyment. Franklyn, however, saw the TV as a resource to engage in his past time: watching movies . . . and more movies. He would lock himself in front of that TV for hours. On many weekends, he remained fixated. It was his new "teaching tool," he would tell anyone within the sound of his voice. He discovered PBS, the only station that provided plays and other artistic productions. There was no HBO. It was a concept not yet invented in those days, so PBS was a station that the artist and the educated and hoi polloi, yes, the common folks that we were, with a penchant for avant garde would tune in. Come Sunday nights, the family traditionally looked at the Ed Sullivan Show. It was the customary thing to do all across America, except for Franklyn who would rather tune in to PBS to indulge his hunt for artistic creativity. He watched performances by actors that one day he dreamed of meeting. He sought inspiration. He learned proper enunciation of words, critiqued their performances, and memorized their parts.

Once again, the brothers butted heads. Their mother, who spent her days toiling for the mighty dollar, had one outlet reserved for her entertainment that came on every Sunday at 8:00 PM. The Ed Sullivan show was a cultural phenomenon that swept the nation, and every household in America tuned to look at this variety show. Franklyn's arrival to the family's tranquility turned everything upside down.

"Franklyn," Lennox would implore, *"we need to watch Ed Sullivan. This is how we do it in this house. We watch the Ed Sullivan show every Sunday."*

"I prefer to watch PBS." Franklyn's response felt like a hard right delivered with full force to my solar plexus, sending my body doubling and my head spinning while gasping for life-saving air.

"You don't understand. Ma wants to watch the Ed Sullivan Show, and I want to watch it, too." I'm feeling a gush of blood rushing to my head, my carotid arteries throbbing with rising anger.

"No, you don't understand, Michael; Sullivan is trite, trivial nonsense, cheap entertainment."

"Look Franklyn . . . I'm telling you . . . this is . . . the only enjoyment Ma has," supplicating.

"No Michael, it has no artistic value, it's entertainment for the masses, mindless . . . pedestrian, besides, PBS offers Tennessee Williams plays that you may come to appreciate."

"Damn Franklyn, that's damn selfish of you . . . and . . . I won't say it again . . ."

"Ok, let him be Michael." At this crucial moment, Ma pipes in diffusing my anger that was boiling tightly contained and about to explode.

Franklyn sits on the sofa in the same spot daily; he paints, eats lots of fruits, drinks juice, eats sandwiches, and overdoses on TV. No one is able to see anything other than what he chooses. Funny enough, he thought that was okay. The sofa finally had a permanent sink hole where he would sit and lie daily. Lennox came to accept that Franklyn's philosophy of life was more important to him than anything he could dare suggest. He had a terrible fierce pride, a wonderful sense of himself Lennox should have seen coming. After all, these traits were self-evident when they were growing up back home but became more pronounced, more discordant as he entered adult life. He came to the only cogent conclusion that he could discern: Franklyn's mind was wired differently than his and all of Olive Seales' children for that matter. He was a unique specimen.

Lennox was already in college by the time Franklyn joined the family in America. He had a job, and driving his own car. The brothers had lots of ground to cover since their separation in 1964. He tried to be his older brother. Oddly enough or should he admit, predictably, that did not work well, so he just settled for brother. He would drive him to Greenwich Village in Washington Square, home of New York University and an enclave of the beat generation where we could comingle with people of all races; the true melting pot. He took him to various parts of Manhattan: Central Park, the Museum of Natural History, St Patrick's Cathedral. They walked the streets where Franklyn began to feel the beat of the city, the rush of traffic, the hurried pedestrians caught in a swirl of activity that will get your head spinning.

He was thrilled by what he saw. Soon he had one of Lennox's subway maps and was riding the iron horse all by himself.

July 12, 1968 marked our daughter's first birthday. Since Franklyn's fell on the 15th, we held a double celebration for his 16th. As he entered our house to join the other guests, Natasha spontaneously flashed a smile. Leslie said, "Look she recognized Franklyn . . ." Our daughter opened her arms as Franklyn lifted her in a wild embrace twirling around sending her into a shrieking giggle.

> "This is Uncle Franklyn, Natasha. Say uncle . . . u-n-c-l-e."
> *"on . . . kol"*
> "Franklyn . . . Frank . . . lyn."
> *"Phan—kin."*
> "That's close enough."

Franklyn dropped to his knees to be at eye level with his niece and the other kids who quickly surrounded him. Some stroking his head, his face. Others jumping on his back. Pretty soon, Franklyn was lying on the floor giddy as can be. Like a kid, he entertained them for hours. At one point, he approached me and began to open up by asking,

> "How did you and Leslie meet?"
> "Well, let's see, I met her when I was an undergraduate student at NYU . . . I was very active in the West Indian Students Association that represented

students from various Caribbean islands. I was one of the organizers of our annual dance that was held at the Loeb Student Center located on the campus in downtown Washington Square I will one day soon take you to see where it is. That evening, I was at the door welcoming our guests when in walks this tall rather attractive girl accompanied by a student with whom I was acquainted on campus. He introduced Leslie as his "cousin." Before she could walk away, I whispered a line that came out of nowhere: *"I hope you will save the last dance for me."* Sure enough, your sister bought it, saved me the dance and the rest, as they say, is history."

"How long after did you get married?"

"A year and a half later we tied the knot . . . not quite two years later Natasha was born, three days before your birthday . . ."

"What about you, Franklyn, what are your plans now that you're finally in New York"?

"Well . . . I don't know yet, but ask me the question a month from now."

"You're turning sixteen in three days. You got to finish high school . . . and . . ."

"Yeah . . . I know . . . I'm gonna find my way. You'll see."

"I'm sure you will acclimate yourself to this new country like Leslie and Michael did before you."

"I'm beginning to like it a lot already."

"Great!"

Two weeks later, Leslie and I, and our daughter came to the house on Carroll street to take Franklyn on his first tour of Manhattan. My brother-in-law recounted the outing with Franklyn:

We drove to Manhattan on that hot summer day: Franklyn seated in the back with Natasha on his lap and speaking non-stop to her. From time to time he would stretch his neck out of the window to admire the skyscrapers pointing to the sky over the city bustling with people. "Wow!" I heard Franklyn exclaim. In this one word, he summarized his unspeakable sense of wonderment. We reached Greenwich Village, the bedrock of the melting pot where I spent my college years, home of artists from all disciplines.

> "Franklyn," I called out to him, "I want you to appreciate the atmosphere of the Village where I'm very positive you will visit very often in the years to come."
> "I'm sure I will." I detected a sound of glee in his voice.

I parked the car and we walked over to an area where the swings were reserved for children and their parents. Franklyn quickly climbed on a slide holding Natasha tightly and slid down. Natasha's giggles signaled she was having a great time with her uncle. This went on for a good hour. "Tell you what Franklyn, the Village is where Leslie and I came often when we were dating. The NYU campus is in the middle of all the activity you see going on day in and day out. You see these outdoor musicians strumming their guitars, singing, others playing chess which is a big pastime among the old timers here, celebrities mingling with the common folk. Back in 1961, I met Richard Pryor who was beginning to make it big on television. Troy Donahue, the heartthrob of our generation came to the Loeb Student Center where he was mobbed by the NYU coeds. Leslie and I went to hear Patty Austin, the great chanteuse, performing in one of the cafes you find here."

"Wow, fascinating!"

"You'll get used to life here which is a lot faster than St Vincent . . ."

"I can tell you right now that I'm loving it already."

We walked back to the car but before we could get in, I noticed a street vendor and invited Franklyn to select a soda.

"Haa! I needed that to cool me off. The heat in New York is humid . . . this is something I will have to get used to."

"You will, you will."

School year began in September. There were a few details Franklyn needed to learn about the school system in America. His mother had contacted the NYC Board of Education and was told to report to Abraham Lincoln High School located on Ocean Parkway. Registration would begin a week prior to the official opening of the school year. Franklyn and his mother left the house very early that Monday morning, walked up Utica Avenue to the Eastern Parkway subway station, a ten minute distance from the house. They boarded the Number 4 train to Franklin Avenue where they exchanged for the Coney Island train and exited at Ocean Parkway, a few yards away from the school. They were greeted by a staff member whose duty was to enroll all new students. Franklyn's school records from St Vincent were presented and met all requirements. Franklyn, however, was to sit for a test that lasted a half hour. Franklyn aced the test and was given the good news to report a week from now to begin his junior year. A guidance counselor was seen the same day to give him the school curriculum. There were elective courses that drew his immediate attention: art classes and the Drama club. These two subjects would soon become his obsession.

He was a quick learner who befriended everyone, soon turning into the typical American teenager while methodically shedding traits of his cultural upbringing. The girls in school were immediately attracted to this transplanted West Indian with the exotic look, product of miscegenation of the races very prevalent in the Caribbean islands. The telephone rang off the hook. His friends were primarily girls he befriended; one in particular by the name of Paula whose parents were educators and resided on Staten Island. He visited them very frequently. By contrast, he did not bring many friends around by the house. He was very circumspect, and uncharacteristically private about allowing people to visit him. He ran into isolation once at home, yet very sociable at school. So, in many ways he was a paradox. He was networking with students and teachers alike to market himself and his talents. He was chosen to headline several theatrical productions at the school. It was obvious to his teachers that they had a raw talent in their hands that needed nurturing.

His brother was in college up town and would often drive him with him to Manhattan to purchase art materials: canvas, brushes, paints. *I had my 1971 VW and drove him to the Village where I introduced him to a few friends. He wasted no time telling me the ones he liked and those I should ignore:*

"Mike, who are these guys you're hanging out with?" He would query.

"What do you mean?"

"These guys don't look like they've got anything to offer you."

"What are you talking about? . . . these guys are my friends."

"Sure, they're your friends . . . going nowhere."

"What do you mean, "going nowhere"? These are nice guys I hang around with . . . they're my friends."

"Sure, they're your friends but I don't think you should be too friendly with them."

This was a line of questioning Lennox did not appreciate coming out of his brother's mouth. Why question the company he chose to keep? It became increasingly infuriating to determine who Franklyn would like in his brother's circle of friends. It was the luck of the draw. He expressed a twisted dislike about them; by and large, young West Indian guys like them, no big ambitions, just good ordinary guys who liked to play guitar and listen to music. But Franklyn saw these friends as people heading "nowhere" in terms of jobs and training. Lennox found his comments cold and cruel. He would habitually put people down for their position and plight. In Lennox's attempt to defend them, Franklyn would not hesitate to put him and them down. However, surprisingly, as the days wore on, Franklyn began to recalibrate his thinking and take things back. In many cases, Lennox had to concede that his little brother was right. It can be said that he had a genuine intolerance for the ordinary, the mundane, the superficial. He saw those friends, if not "losers", quite likely on their way to oblivion. Therein lay the difference between the two of them. Lennox enjoyed the city while staying true to his Caribbean culture. Franklyn by contrast was always striving to move out and make his escape. It takes two to fight, so he spewed these negative statements and that was that. Lennox could not present a legitimate defense. He did not allow him time to do it. He found myself at the losing end of the battles of egos. This, by the way, never stopped. *"He dared tell me that he saw me as 'ordinary and truly heading nowhere.' Me. He dared challenge with his numbskull absurdity. I constructed my life where I embraced the culture of the welcoming land while always trying to blend and share as I traveled. The schism grew deeper and sharper, yet much later in this evolutionary process, Franklyn and I arrived at a juncture where the gap grew much narrower. We could enjoy each other's company and laugh, albeit it required much work to get to those places of surrender and acceptance."*

Franklyn was always the actor trapped in a role of his fertile imagination hence compelled to seek conflict before getting to the underlying truth. He was never content to be "nice" in their day to day relationship. He felt a compelling need to go beyond the surface and to dig deeper and by provoking dissention, assume control. On some rare occasions, they would come to a place in their daily interactions where they reached common ground, but Lennox naive optimism would be short lived again because Franklyn would construe these moments of perceived weakness on his brother's part to renew his challenge and dissect his reaction as he got unglued, deteriorating into a heated argument. Lennox would reach a point where he would swear him off of his life and tell him to "go to hell." The next day would come and he would greet him with a waterfall of laughter and say, "I had a good time last night Michael" inviting him for another get together. "What the #$%!*?" *"Only a brief few hours had passed since I was almost ready to choke him, yet he was now acting as if nothing untoward had happened between us. I was supposed to accept that his outbursts were chimerical, forget the anger he caused me, and move on. He would walk past me whistling a happy tune before I was able to register a reaction. As far as he was concerned, 'Yesterday is but a memory, today is the moment at hand, deal with it,' he would often say."* This pattern was one that occurred over and over between them. Lennox had to be aware that Franklyn was truly an actor first and foremost. He acted on and off cue. Lennox would premeditatively suppress that part of him, hoping that it was just two guys or two brothers interacting. Such was not the case. The actor in him had predominance. So essentially, the actor was never far away from him. It was the conduit by which everyone met him on his terms. Much later, he came to acknowledge that behavior, not regret it, but accept it as a part of the process of staying true to his raison d'être, that which defines him.

Franklyn liked everything he saw in Manhattan: the buildings, the food that catered to all palates, the museums, the parks. They would walk together around Broadway where he became fascinated with the theater district. Lennox would also take him to hang out with a few of his friends in Brooklyn Heights overlooking the Manhattan skylines and the Hudson River. The fast pace of city life attracted him from the get go. One could interpret the excitement in his eyes wherever they went. It was a multi-developmental process of one coming to terms with living away from the Caribbean, shaking off the confines of the close-knit culture in Brooklyn. He saw a path that led him to move beyond the comfort and the boundaries of being safe at home, eating West Indian foods and sitting around making small talk. He was not content to be absorbed into this Island safety net in Brooklyn. He reached out and stretched himself towards his dreams and yearnings.

Then came a new season unfamiliar to Franklyn except from books they read growing up in the tropics that yielded eternal summers. Winter had arrived and unlike many Caribbean natives who suffer the first blast of cold air, Franklyn embraced it with the bravura of a matador.

One day, his school friends invited him to Rockefeller Center for an introduction to ice skating. Did he know anything about ice skating? Of course not, but that did not stop Franklyn who loved to test his limits. He did not do too well, you see. That's an understatement. The Olympic skater, Brian Boitano, he was not. Overlooking the fact that he was never near an ice rink as a child, he nevertheless jumped into the deep end of that rink. Of course the speed of the experienced skaters allowed very little tolerance for the green skater. It was not a place for the faint of heart. Not to be denied and responding to the encouragement from his friends, he donned a pair of skates and away he went, his legs taking off under him in a vertical trajectory toward the sky precipitating an awkward fall on his back with one fragile leg absorbing the full impact of his weight against the hard ice. His first experience with ice skating was, to say the least, a major disaster. He broke the leg. The ambulance came and rushed him to Mount Sinai hospital to realign the fractured tibia and to put the leg in a cast. He returned home that evening accompanied by two of his classmates, Jeff and Isaac, helping him negotiate the stairs leading to the second floor apartment. At the sight of him, Ma let out a scream:

> "Franklyn, what happened to you?" she bellowed through the open door, into the street, attracting the neighbors' attention.
> "It's ok Ma . . . I'll be alright," Franklyn replied, trying to reassure her.

"But how did you hurt yourself . . . what happened to your leg?" Ma pressed her interrogation, beginning to hyperventilate.

"I'll be ok Ma . . . calm down . . . I'll be ok."

"Lord of Mercy . . . tell me what happened . . . Jeff . . . Isaac . . . what happened?"

"Ok Ma . . . we all went ice skating at Rockefeller Center and I had a little accident . . . that's all."

"You call this . . . a little accident Franklyn . . . Lord of Mercy?" she asked, looking at the two crutches he placed next to him as he sat. Mrs. Seales' blood pressure must have shot up at this point, but she gradually recovered from this unexpected shock.

For days Franklyn limped around on crutches. Speaking of one who takes his role seriously, "Break a leg" is the idiom used among actors before they go on stage. He took his call quite literally. Nothing slowed him down, though. The art classes afforded him full expression of his creativity as a young man in pursuit of a dream that heretofore was not taken seriously or perhaps misunderstood by the family. At the end of his first school year we were invited to a school production of McBeth's Romeo and Juliet that gave him exposure to his budding career. The stage was his calling, and he had finally found his niche.

Days, weeks and months followed; Franklyn worked assiduously at reinventing himself. He knew he had to find a middle of the road accent, so television became his vehicle. He would have marathon sessions in front of the TV, learning to speak the American accent yet heavily influenced by British erudition. He went to the movies, art exhibits, and plays. He was networking and going out with a classmate we knew by the name of Paula. It never failed to amaze me how Franklyn was such a natural with finding his way around the city. He had a good sense of travel and was ready for the big time.

Though the theatre was his obsession, he also kept a drawing pad close by wherever he traveled to record an idea, a scenery of kind, one of hundreds of things that flooded his imagination. When we asked him to show us, he would display his work though he guarded jealously. Describing his sketches and paintings was not a task that fell to the amateur. It was obvious to me that he was a student of the Master, one of the most dynamic and influential artists of our century: Pablo Picasso. Some of Franklyn's paintings captured the mood of melancholy and isolation with his choice of somber colors, while others were draped with vibrant hues of the rainbow influenced no doubt by his Caribbean heritage, the mystic indigenous people who populated his village.

When asked to describe his paintings, he would effusively say:

> *"I would like you to perceive my art as something of nature that can heal with its color, its movement and its simplicity".*
>
> *"I love color. I also love the radiograph. I found that pen and really fell in love with it. It creates those lines that I want that segment the body . . . to treat the body not as an inhuman thing, but to see if I could*

> *make something human out of something that was sort of angular. But mostly, I'm interested in a lot of color, a lot of vibrancy: nature! And, I'm not very interested in painting reality, per se. I'm representing reality, in color, in form, in line: in black and white and in color . . ."*
>
> *"This is my dream. To get better, buy an old cottage or something . . . somewhere, have some dogs, paint and live out the rest of my days happy . . ."*

By his senior year in high school, Franklyn had become a sought after performer in his school productions, headlining numerous plays where he displayed his acting versatility, delivering his lines with perfect erudition, while also exhibiting his dancing and singing with equal aplomb. Two months before graduation, his girlfriend, Paula, who also had dreams of pursuing an acting career asked him to accompany her to the famed Juilliard School for the Performing Arts in Manhattan to help with her audition. Franklyn had on occasions talked to his brother about fashion design. Both he and Paula shared the aspiration of attending the famed Parsons School of Design upon graduation. It was a second option he contemplated while devoting much effort to his budding acting career, given they were both very active in the drama club in high school and had been in more than one production, he told no one that he was going to accompany Paula to her audition at Juilliard. Franklyn casually tagged along totally oblivious of the destiny that awaited him. Upon their arrival, they were greeted by none other than the legendary director, producer, actor, John Houseman who asked Franklyn,

"Are you here to audition also?" Caught by surprise, Franklyn naively muttered, "NO, sir, I' m here for my friend . . . we rehearsed the balcony scene from "Romeo and Juliet." She wants to act it out . . . I'm only here for the ride."

"I see," responded Mr. Houseman, taking Franklyn at his word.

Fate intervened at a most auspicious time upon Mr. Houseman's insistence who said, "I will observe you and critique how both you and your friend do."

"Yes sir, I will do my best," Franklyn responded deadpan.

The audition lasted approximately fifteen minutes during which Mr. Houseman and his assistant's attentions were drawn to Franklyn emoting his lines to perfection. Mr. Houseman was so captivated by the ease, the movement, the delivery of the lines that with much effusion whispered to his assistant that his instinct told him he may have discovered a diamond in the rough. Mr. Houseman asked Franklyn to step into his tastefully decorated office with pictures of legends of the arts draping the walls. Franklyn hesitantly followed, feeling his heart pounding heavily in his chest, his thoughts racing.

"Take a seat, young man." Franklyn is motioned to a chair facing Mr. Houseman's glass-covered desk which, except for the notes he took during the audition, was bare.

"How do you think you did?" Mr. Houseman asks Franklyn with a concealed smile.

"Well, Sir, I did my best." Franklyn answers hesitantly.

"Franklyn, you told me you did not come for an audition, but rather to help your friend, is that correct?"

"Err, Um . . . yes Sir, I did say that."

"Young man, how would you like to pursue an acting career in this institution?"

"Excuse me . . . err . . . Mr. Houseman . . . I must say this would be nice . . . but my family can't afford the tuition . . . that would be impossible, Sir."

"Franklyn, you don't understand what I just said. I didn't ask you if your parents can afford to send you here. Young man, I see great potential in you and I'm offering you a full scholarship to Juilliard beginning this upcoming school term."

"What!?" "What did you say?" "Did you say . . . ?"

"Yes, you heard me correctly . . ."

"Mr. Houseman . . . excuse me to interrupt . . . but . . . I don't know what to say . . . I mean, thank you . . . this is unbelievable . . ."

Not one to communicate with an economy of words, Franklyn's response at that moment had lost coherence under the influence of potent emotions that were not easily restrained.

"That's okay, Franklyn. You will receive a letter of confirmation and all pertinent directives for matriculation. Congratulations!"

"Thank you sir . . . thank you . . . thank you!"

Franklyn stands up and grabs the hand Mr. Houseman offers to him and hops out of the office, flashing a big grin that is easily spotted by his friend Paula.

Like a hound, Mr. Houseman had a nose for talents he could mold into the super stars of tomorrow. Franklyn was offered a full four year scholarship on the spot. He was dumbfounded, overwhelmed by what he had just heard from this legendary impresario. Ironically and sadly, his companion was not chosen; however, she loved him so much, they remained friends until his death. Studying Franklyn's metamorphosis from his childhood days to the theatre stage became fodder for those competing for his attention and wondering why he seemed always on the go. The poem by Robert Frost comes to mind, which may perhaps shed some light: *"The woods are lovely, dark and deep, but I have promises to keep, and miles to go before I sleep . . ."* Franklyn was only on the threshold of a promising career in the theatre that is reserved only for the select. He had a long road ahead strewn with twists and turns and pitfalls that would discourage lesser mortals; nevertheless, he followed it with total abandonment and self-assurance. At graduation time he was cast to play Don Quixote from the Broadway play, "Man of La

Mancha." Franklyn gave an outstanding performance that confirmed that his star was rising.

"Destiny" is defined as a "concept based on the belief that there is a fixed natural order to the cosmos . . . a fixed sequence of events that is inevitable and unchangeable." Franklyn had met his on that day. Some on the other hand might also call it "Luck" which is "a matter of preparation meeting opportunity."

It matters not which definition one chooses, Franklyn Seales was heading for Juilliard, a far cry from Calliaqua.

It did not take Franklyn long to firmly conclude that Brooklyn was no longer his launching pad. He felt alienated in that borough. His objective was to network and be totally absorbed in city life, i.e. the theater district, the restaurants, the fast pace and all the nuances in which he could indulge himself. So, when he completed his first semester at Julliard, he told me that the moment that he had dreamt many times had arrived. He was ready to pull out of Brooklyn. He and fellow students at Juilliard had found an apartment on the upper West Side at 120 West 82nd Street. Among his roommates, I discovered, was an unknown Robin Williams who everyone with a pulse recognized would become a huge super star of stage, television and the movies. One Sunday, Lennox gathered his belongings, packed them in a rental truck and away they went to Manhattan. Lennox engaged him in small talk knowing full well that this separation from the family was of his own choosing.

"How many of you will be living in the apartment?" breaking the monotonous silence.

"The five of us will be sharing a three bedroom apartment."

"Not bad, must be a big apartment . . . how big are the rooms?"

"Big enough for us" almost dismissing me and the question.

"Anyone know how to cook?" I asked in jest.

"We'll do just fine. I know how to boil water" he said half jokingly.

"I'm sure Lessie taught you at least that, right?, trying to bring some levity in our conversation.

"Can you go a little faster, Mike?"

"Sure, but you don't want us to get a ticket . . . in another fifteen minutes or so we'll be there."

They pulled up in front of a towering apartment building. They were greeted by the doorman who instructed them to use the service elevator to haul Franklyn's belongings. From this day forward he was now a man of "Gotham," the "Big Apple," no longer having to ride the iron horse for Brooklyn to and fro, free to live his life without parental and brotherly interference in the belly of the "Naked City."

Attending Juilliard was the epitome, the seminal moment, the dream of every budding actor of consequence. Among the graduates we can count Christine Baranski, William Hurt, Kevin Kline, Mandy Patankin, Kevin Spacey, Kelly McGillis, Ving Rhames, who went on to achieve national recognition, and the list goes on and on, to be added was Franklyn Vincent Ellison Seales. We knew then that he had fastened his blinders securely and was looking straight forward. No looking back for him.

The significance of Franklyn's winning a scholarship to Juilliard did not hit his brother right away. He experienced a delayed reaction to the realization that rushed to overwhelm him once he began to reflect on the history of this unique American school. The Drama Division where Franklyn's talent was best suited was founded in 1968 by the renowned American director, producer, and theater administrator John Houseman with whom Franklyn had a serendipitous chance encounter and the French director, teacher, and actor Michel Saint-Denis. Mr. Houseman and Saint-Denis, we learned, *devised a four-year curriculum based upon the training methods Saint-Denis and his wife, Suria, had devised for their European and Canadian conservatories. Still in use today, these guidelines provide actors with a disciplined framework through which to explore the depths of their own creativity.* Reading Juilliard's Mission *". . . to provide the highest caliber of artistic education for gifted musicians, dancers, and actors from around the world, so that they may achieve their fullest potential as artists, leaders, and global citizens,"* began to somewhat put things in perspective as we followed Franklyn's immersion into this world that growing up on the tiny island, we could not possibly have envisioned. "Only in America" indeed, made more sense than ever. These were not empty words. Franklyn's stratospheric rise will prove that dreams do materialize for those who dare.

Franklyn invited Lennox to meet him at the school one day and as he recalled: *"I can never, nor would I want to ever forget the experience of walking in this multi-story home in Lincoln Center for the first time. Located in an expensive environment of NYC: Columbus Circle, The Philharmonic Hall, Central Park and all of the great hotels a few blocks away, The Plaza, The Ritz. It was profoundly exhilarating.*

"Classrooms were on the first floor, second and third floors, not the typical classrooms. There were lots of partitions that were movable. Small stages to larger stages, easily adjustable depending on the demand and purpose were scattered throughout. He walked me into this establishment, as I gawked at rows of pictures and art works of renowned artists lining the walls. Students and faculty members milled around on stages where one could see actors rehearsing their lines for the next drama presentations, dancers caught in leaps that defy gravity, the sound of music reverberating in the halls. What seemed almost like a bombardment on the senses had fluidity and purpose. Franklyn introduced me to his professors, friends and classmates. He was in his element and was admired and appreciated by his peers."

Once a week they would meet in the city always eager to share his latest adventure and at times go out to grab something to eat. On this particular encounter that will perhaps be memorialized in a future play for its challenge to Lennox's sensibilities and manhood, he chose to "go Chinese."

"We sauntered to one restaurant located three blocks away from Lincoln Center, were seated and after putting our order in, a mix of egg foo yong and "general Tso" we intend to share, we await for the order to be served while we engage in a conversation focused more on the dynamics of the city that suited him well. The order is brought to our table. "Looks great!" I opined. After taking the first bite, Franklyn says, "Michael, I don't like this food . . . have them bag it, and we'll go look for another restaurant." My food tastes just fine, I thought, but he leaves me with no choice in the decision and I obediently follow him out of the restaurant hauling two bags of freshly cooked food. We leave in search of another establishment nearby. He points to an Italian restaurant. It's an upscale one that has tables draped with cloth and padded dark crimson chairs. The cutlery is of the finest quality. The walls are adorned with reproductions of paintings from the Masters: Da Vinci, Michelangelo, Raphael, Picasso, Toulouse-Lautrec, Van Gogh and others. Framed autographed pictures of celebrities who sat at those tables spoke of class, catering to the higher ups on the food chain. An unobtrusive sign on the wall reveals the restaurant accommodates no more than 200 patrons; men dressed in suit and tie, women in their fine designer clothes that draw admiring stares from the connoisseurs. We arrive at a time it is very much filled to its capacity. We are greeted by the maitre d' who politely leads us to a table midway of the room near a window decorated with expensive embroidered drapes that accentuate the refinement of the restaurant. The waiter hands us a leather, I repeat, a soft leather bound menu. It smells of leather. Yes, imprinted in the lower back is the word 'cowhide.' I'm impressed. "Would you like to start with an *aperitif, gentlemen?" the waiter inquires in his accented English that betrays his European origin. I select the house Merlot. "Good choice, sir" I hear him confirm. "How about you sir?" turning to Franklyn whose index finger gesture signals a "no." "I'll be right back with your drink while you gentlemen select your order." My eyes wander around the room to see everyone understandably enjoying their selected dishes and conversing in animated tones. We hear the sudden pop of a Champagne bottle followed by voices of approval from two couples celebrating a semi-private occasion. Franklyn chooses a dish of shrimp scampi on a bed of angel hair spaghetti I trust he will surely enjoy. I nod to the waiter to make it the same for me while I take a sip of the Merlot he places before me. While waiting for the much anticipated meal, I nervously if not contemptuously fill in the dead air by reminiscing about our childhood days. Franklyn abruptly interrupts me and speaks of his Juilliard experience . . . Fair enough.*

"Tell you what, Michael, I have to sometimes pinch myself to believe I'm not dreaming. Tell me the truth . . . did you ever think . . . I would one day . . . be a student at Julliard . . . a school I never heard of before coming to the U.S.?"

Franklyn sounded as if he were measuring every word for effect.
"Err . . ."
"Come on Mike, hear this. Just three years ago . . . I was living in Calliaqua . . . without a clue what America was all about . . .

Here I am now Mike . . . studying at Julliard . . . J-u-l-l-i-a-r-d Mike . . . Wow!!!Come on dude . . . speak to me."

Franklyn's voice was becoming more animated as he peppered me with his questions.

"I see what you mean but . . ."

"But what, Mike? Do you have any idea how many great artists graduated from this school?

"Err . . . I dunno."

"Never mind . . . I tell you what. I will be one of their graduates. You Just watch me Mike . . . Just watch."

"I guess you will . . ."

"What do you mean "guess"? I'm telling you. I will graduate from Juilliard. I know it . . . I can feel it."

"Yes Franklyn, YOU WILL . . . damn dude, take it easy, will ya."

"Yes siree bob! I can feel it . . . everything is going my way . . . no question about it."

"Yep, you're doing great . . ."

"You bet I'm doing great."

"Excuse me gentlemen."

Our conversation is abruptly interrupted by the waiter bringing us our order, not a minute too soon before Franklyn drives me nuts. Without hesitation, I dive into my plate. I'm on my third scoop before Franklyn starts with his first and I'll be darn If I don't hear his grumble:

"I don't like this. Damn! That food doesn't taste right. Let's bag it Mike."

I swallow a half chewed mouthful and call out:

"*Hold it right there Franklyn,*" *cautiously not raising my voice to unnecessarily draw attention to me, I say:*

"*Come on dude . . . this is no frickin' ordinary restaurant . . . this is good stuff, Franklyn . . . this dish tastes great . . . come on try, eat the damn food, will you . . .*" *biting my lips in a futile attempt to contain my boiling anger. Once again Franklyn shakes his head disapprovingly and makes his point clear:*

"*Let's go! Ask the waiter to bag the food,*" *he said with a willfulness in his eyes.*

Away we go in search of another restaurant I am prayerfully hoping might satisfy Franklyn's discriminating taste buds. I am beginning to get real irritated and muttered,

"*How stupid of me to follow him to lunch!*" "*How about some Greek food Michael?*" *I hear him not exactly ask, rather tell me in a tone that clearly says, I have no choice.* "*Sure why not . . . Let's go!*" *I could not say no . . . Are you crazy? I seriously doubt my words can make a difference, him being the stubborn, obstinate man that he is. By this time I am convinced he has made up his mind to eat the doggone food. I am beginning to feel hunger pangs that could have been easily satiated an hour ago. The waiter approaches and hands us the menus. The gesture with my open right hand signals to the waiter to keep mine. I eye Franklyn and let him order.*

"*What will you have Mike?*" *he asks.*

"*Go 'head, order something, anything, I'll eat the same, it's your call.*" *I respond. His eyes narrow as he detects the biting irritation in my voice, but quickly dismisses it. I let him do the ordering while getting more agitated by the second.*

My stomach lets out a growl that no doubt could be heard by patrons seated at the table next to ours. An awkward silence hangs in the air while we wait for the food. I occasionally glance at him to see if I can recognize a facial expression that yielded a clue of sort. The waiter finally brings a platter of astako makaronada he wheels on a tray from which he fills our plates. With a name like, "astako makaronada," or "Lobster Pasta" it's got to be good, right? Well, at the very least, I thought. Since Franklyn ordered it, he should eat it, I mutter under my breath. At this point, my mouth is drooling and can't wait. I reach for the napkin to wipe my chin of the saliva that drips on my shirt. The plate placed before me looks delicious with an aroma that surely can seduce the most demanding palate, confirmed after the first bite. Franklyn however almost spit out his first nibble and immediately stands up and once again commands,

"Bag it!!!"

I stare at this actor first and brother second only to have him staring back unblinking ready to tell me again that he was right and I was wrong. I lower my eyes, then defiantly explode:

"What's going on Franklyn?#@$?" I hear me barking at him.

"Let's go Michael," he calmly responds.

"I can't believe this crap." I hurl at him. "What's wrong with you?"

Patrons seated at nearby tables are distracted by the tone of my voice, loud enough to be heard a good twenty feet away. They stare at two guys who they must think the police should be called to haul away in their paddy wagon. I didn't care at this point.

"Nothing is wrong with me Michael . . ." he says in a very controlled tone.

"So, why don't you sit down and eat the damn frickin' food," I bark right back.

"Let's go Mike."

"Shiiiiit!" I throw my hands in the air, disgusted. I briskly gesture to the waiter to come over. He trots to our table, looks at us with a hurried expression that begs for an explanation.

"Anything wrong gentlemen?" he asks

"Nothing is wrong, we have to leave . . . the bill please." Franklyn offers an unconvincing reply.

"Bull s***" I mutter. I am mad as hell as we walk out, my face contorted and clenched like a fist. As we hit the outside air, I grab him by the arm and spin him around.

"What the FN hell is wrong with you? We stopped at three different restaurants and you pulled the same bull crap . . . what kind of game are you playing Franklyn?"

My words have no effect on him. He pulls back. His face remains stoic, and he cavalierly dismisses my rant. He doesn't hear a word. He shuts me off. At this point, I tell him,

"I'm heading home back to Brooklyn where us ordinary folks don't go through that kind of drama just to eat food . . ."

We're the unsophisticated plebeians. I know he believes we are. Our lunch date, as one can easily surmise, was a disaster of tsunamic proportion to say the very least. I drive home understandably dejected, hauling six bags of food. For the next few days I reflect on Franklyn's overly dramatic rejection of the meals he ordered from three different good restaurants. I remained mystified and never once dared question his motivation. I was certain of one thing: his explanation would be constructed to bolster his already inflated ego, a petty talent tied to vanity.

I should at least feel content or privileged no doubt—as I believe he thinks-that he was inviting me to school productions in which he was cast in a variety of characters, from serious Shakespearean plays to light comedies, showcasing his nimble versatility. I was happier to remain on the sidelines of his world which he cultivated with a burning passion and steadfastness that I must admit fascinated and intrigued me to the nth degree. He kept me spellbound speaking of celebrities he met, actors and actresses he admired from afar but who have now become members of his growing circle of friends. If there were any doubts about his future success, listening to him would quell one's trepidation. He was not unlike Muhammad Ali who challenged our imaginations with his nom de guerre: "I'm the greatest!!!" Franklyn, I would say, came from the same mindset that exudes supreme confidence in his God-given gift that transcends the mundane, the hum drum world in which the rest of us function.

At his next visit to Juilliard, Lennox watched him being tutored the sport of fencing, a skill he needed to master when called to play a particular Shakespearean role. He told him how much he likes it; though new to him, he learned it very quickly. At yet another visit, he observed him taking voice lessons. Here again Franklyn displayed extraordinary versatility. These skills were second nature to him whose mettle was tested in his very first year at Juilliard being chosen to appear in several productions: "A View from the Bridge" by Arthur

Miller. "The Kitchen" by Arnold Wesker. "Chips with Everything," also by Arnold Wesker. "Ah Wilderness" by Eugene O'Neill. "The Taming of the Shrew" by William Shakespeare. "Camino Real" by Tennessee Williams, and several others that won the approval of producers who routinely visited Juilliard in search of promising talents. Franklyn was on their radar screen and kept on a short list of actors wanted in future productions.

After four years spent in the crucible of an actor's life Franklyn's graduation in 1974 was anticlimactic. Theories set aside, he knew the parchment given to him was no gold key to the kingdom of Hollywood, yet he was appreciative of his serendipitous acceptance at the school, the training and applied discipline learned. He was faced with the reality that an actor is like a good carpenter given a blueprint, he builds to meet the exact specs through applied knowledge, sweats and tears. He knew hard work brings life to the spoken word, though confronted with adversity he was nevertheless confident of the outcome. Graduation had the appearance of an epic event. His graduating class from the Drama Department was rather small by comparison to the other disciplines. He was one among the select few. his mother, Regis, Debbie and Lennox witnessed the pageantry unfolding, mesmerized by the magic of the day. They were greeted by his student friends and his professors who told his mother how proud she must be of her son who made a huge impression on them.

September 1975 came and Lennox's decision to get married did not surprise anyone within the family. He'd been courting Juanita, one of three daughters of Rosey and Quincy Smith, their neighbors whose house stood opposite ours on East 59th Street in Brooklyn, the house he had purchased three years before after leaving their apartment on Carroll street. He chose Franklyn to be his best man and Juanita selected her friend, Jillian, as Maid of Honor. They were acquainted with a minister who lived in Queens who told them that if they were willing to come to his house by 8:00 AM, he would marry them. They decided that it was as good an offer as any. They already had secured the marriage license in downtown Brooklyn at the bureau that issued these licenses. So early that morning, Lennox chose to wear a shirt and slacks. Franklyn did the same and Juanita, dressed in a simple but fashionable white dress, had only to walk across the street where Franklyn, Jillian, and Lennox piled up in a red Firebird belonging to his sister's boyfriend, Neville, and drove to the Queens address. He was humbled by Franklyn's willingness to take time off from his busy actor's life and join them in the most important decision of their lives. Here were the two brothers on their way to the wedding. *"We had no money but we were full of hope,"* recalls Lennox. The Firebird took them to the house where Mrs. Schmedes invited them into her living room while her husband, Leslie the Minister, was still in the shower. A few minutes pass, then, in walks their host where they are restlessly waiting. He greets them dressed in his white Tee shirt, grey slacks and barefoot. After exchanging a few pleasantries they hear him ask, "Are you guys ready?" *"As ready as we'll ever be,"* Lennox mutters in a trembling voice. "OK, you two kneel before me and you two are the bridesmaid and the best man? Now, I want you two to stand behind them." *"Kneeling on the hard wooden floor sends shock waves to my knee caps and up my back."* Lennox recalls. With Franklyn and Jillian flanking them as witnesses, in five minutes, he pronounces them, "Man and Wife."

Leaving the Minister's house, Franklyn makes them a generous offer: "Mike," he says, "let's drive into Manhattan where we will eat breakfast together." In a flash they were off from Queens to Mid-town Manhattan for a restaurant on the Upper West Side. The girls settled for sandwiches while Franklyn and Lennox chewed on their breakfast of bacon and eggs with toast, washed down with Lipton tea. It was Lennox's first meal with his new wife of less than two hours. After leaving the restaurant, they proceed to drop Franklyn at his Manhattan apartment, and continue on to Brooklyn, first dropping Jillian home then back to their apartment at Jodie Court.

"I was rather astonished at Franklyn's willingness to be with me on my most important day. It was very humbling and so unlike him. However, He was right there when I needed him and we had a nice quiet time. No fuss, no fight, no cross words; things could not have been more salubrious," Lennox pensively recalls.

Barely a few days after their marriage as they settled into their new apartment at Jodie Court, Franklyn paid them a visit to present them with two of his paintings as wedding gifts. They knew that money was very tight, so he commissioned himself to complete two pictures which he did in pen and ink. He also matted the paintings, framed, and brought them over to the apartment. Lennox was impressed, to say the least. He kept them company long enough to help them hang his art work. Thirty five years later Lennox has those two paintings on his walls in his Pooler office. It was a super generous thing to do. It was not long after he began marriage life that he heard that Franklyn was seriously contemplating leaving New York after completing some theatre engagements to pursue his dreams in Tinsel Town, Hollywood.

Franklyn honed his craft appearing in plays with a young then unknown classmate, Christine Baranski who later went on to achieve enormous success on Broadway, in television and the movies. Franklyn and Christine were both cast in "'Tis Pity She's A Whore" at the Goodman Theatre in 1975. A critic wrote *"As the two lovers, Christine Baranski and Franklyn Seales display considerably more than just heir handsome young bodies. They perform with poise and passion that do credit to their training as recent graduates of the Juilliard School of Drama in New York City."* He continued to appear regularly in off Broadway productions where he soon captured the attention of the celebrated American theatrical producer and director, Joseph Papp, who cast him in his Shakespeare in the Park productions. By this time, Franklyn Seales of Calliaqua had morphed into an authentic Shakespearian actor speaking in a crisp British accent, performing in Papp's Hamlet in which he played the role of Fortinbras, Prince of Norway. Other members of the cast included Robert Burr, Ruby Dee, John Lithgow, Sam Waterston, actors who became household names. He was cast in Romeo and Juliet, Othello, King Lear, the Tempest and several other productions. The uncanny transformation was complete and mystified his relatives who grew up with him never anticipating success would come knocking at his door so quickly at the age of 23. The ebullience of the family was perfectly captured by our comments following Franklyn's performances. He counted among his friends the great actor of stage, television and movies, the man gifted with an easily recognizable mellifluous voice, James Earl Jones who he knew simply as "Jimmy." Wow, From Calliaqua to Juilliard was a straight line for this son of St Vincent. It bears repeating: "Preparation meeting opportunity."

In 1974, Franklyn's younger brother, Raymond more popularly called, Reggie, by family and friends, had left Saint Vincent to join the other members of the family in Brooklyn. One day, Reggie received a call from his brother inviting him to a production that will be performed in Central Park under the direction of the legendary, Joseph Papp, the founder of "Shakespeare in the Park" productions. Franklyn was cast as a member of the play Hamlet scheduled that early July evening in the open air stage.

"Franklyn introduced me to some members of the cast," recalls Reggie, *"as I got myself comfortable to watch him in action. All was going well until three quarters of an hour into the play when we suddenly hear thunder and lightning flashing. The sky opened up and a torrential rain cascaded on the crowd, chasing everyone to run for cover. I see all the actors scurrying under a large tent that can shelter a good hundred people. I move closer to Franklyn making sure security doesn't tell me to get out.*

Everybody is laughing and taking the interruption in stride. At one point I watch Franklyn moving to another corner of the tent leaving me to wait up for the rain to stop. Then from the corner of my eyes I catch a group of male actors shedding their wet clothes, thinking perhaps they were changing to dry ones. What followed however was unpredictable and caught me by surprise. These men, I counted twenty of them, including Franklyn went streaking in the rain buck naked like junior high school kids being hose around a fire hydrant to the delight of their fellow actors and a few people in the crowd that remained although an announcement was made that the show was cancelled."

Franklyn's roles were garnering recognition among the glitterati, the habitués of Broadway and off-Broadway productions. The family began to see less and less of him, unless for an occasional call to his mother to reaffirm his love for her, notwithstanding the contentious relationship that still persisted, and to say hello to everyone. King Lear was made for TV in 1974 and he played a minor role as the servant of Cornwall. In 1977 he appeared in a play, "A Very Private Life", starring Celeste Holm, the seasoned actress of film, television and the stage. A theatre critic wrote:

"The only other character in the play is the houseboy. Franklyn Seales plays this important part, wearing Gucci shoes and forty dollar shirts. According to this play he walked in one day in need of work and food and just stayed. His duties include those of servant, secretary, and

bartender. It's a good thing that he decided to stay when he did. He is a plus to this strong but small cast."

In 1974, Franklyn was cast in "The Tempest" for which he continued to receive glorious reviews:

"Franklyn Seales is a soaring Ariel. He is particularly good vocally, and since Ariel has some of the play's most glorious language, this is a great asset. Visually he owes a lot to modern dance. His costume seemed to have been borrowed from one of Martha Graham's Greek gods, a web of ropes barely covering his nakedness. His makeup and movements are reminiscent of Nijinsky as the faun in "Afternoon of a Faun."

It was, however, in 1978 that he was introduced to the nation when he clinched the lead role in "Trial of the Moke" based on the real life story of the humiliation and anguish suffered by Lt. Henry Ossian Flipper, the first black graduate of West Point. Assigned to serve at Fort Davis, Texas in 1881, Flipper became the object of a conspiracy to rid the base of its only black graduate. Flipper, portrayed by Franklyn Seales, was framed by white officers who accused him of embezzling government funds. Ninety-four years later, Flipper was vindicated only a week after "The Trial of the Moke" ended its world premiere run at the Milwaukee Repertory Theater in 1976. A military reburial with honors followed in 1978.

The fact that Franklyn was selected to play the role of Lt. Henry Flipper, the principal character of the play, was a welcomed opportunity but not fortuitous.

Notwithstanding the physical resemblance between him and Lt Flipper which was uncanny, but far more telling was the confidence he had generated for the producers to select him based on the mastery of his craft, his superb stage presence. One critic wrote, *"Seales carries the weight of the play's message, but he keeps the drama under control, resisting the temptation to push the message by "emoting" for dramatic effect. Instead, he portrays Henry Flipper with the dignity and self-respect which were his due."* His appearance on national television sent a swell of pride through the family gathered to watch Franklyn deliver a masterful performance. The question we ask ourselves: should we act so surprised at his almost meteoric rise to national notoriety? He would be the first to answer, "I knew it all along . . ." Yeah, he knew it all along alright. Who would dare deny him his inherent drives to succeed in his chosen profession.

When we allow ourselves to flip backward to the times Franklyn and Lennox were growing up on Labourne street in the tiny village of Calliaqua, one is overwhelmed by present realities, unable to reconcile these two divergent, conflicting worlds. One that offered Franklyn no opportunities except to escape into an fantasy world that only he knew existed in the profundity of his imagination. Only he could construct this world that would become manifest once he set foot in America. *"Nothing prepared me to witness my brother's accomplishments. In fact, it would be highly presumptuous of me to claim otherwise. We can liken his evolution to the birth of a butterfly that goes through a metamorphosis from the tiny egg to the caterpillar, to the chrysalis before reaching full maturity and flying away to dazzle our eyes and our imaginations, only to fly too close to the sun, and burn and crash like Icarus,"* This was the quintessential Franklyn, the vulnerable man/boy imbued with a "Je ne sais quoi" dealing with life as very few can, but alas soaring too high only to fall victim of his excesses. He exhibited an air of sophistication, an elegance, a refinement that could charm a listener yet at times project a tackiness that could wear out one's welcome. It is this dichotomy that sets him so far apart from the common man. He was a rare breed artist carved from the Hairoun rocks of his ancestry into a shining star that dimmed too early.

Franklyn's brilliant performance in the "Trial of the Moke" must have triggered a strong ripple effect to reach Hollywood because it was not long after his televised performance that we heard he was packing his belongings and heading west to Tinsel Town, to the land of make believe, where stars are born and dreams remain unfulfilled, victims of broken promises. The year was 1979 when the movie, "The Onion Field" was released, an adaptation of the book by Joseph Wambaugh. "It's the in-depth analysis of the true story of a 1963 event in Los Angeles. Two cops pull over two crooks in an otherwise routine traffic stop. But the desperate crooks get the drop on the cops, get their guns, kidnap them, drive them out to an onion field in the countryside, and murder one of them. One of the cops escapes death, but is haunted by guilt over the death of his partner and his inability to help. The murderers are captured, tried, convicted, and then retried over and over again on appeal." Here we have Franklyn playing the role of Jimmy Lee Smith aka Jimmy

Youngblood, a petty thief along with his companion Gregory Ulas Powell played by James Woods, another up and coming very talented actor.

By this time, Franklyn had taken permanent residence in California. He was living "La Vida Loca." We suspected he had fully espoused the seductive, runaway decadent life style of Hollywood, the land of permissive pleasures that swallowed him in a dizzying swirl of fast women, fast cars, sexual encounters of the forbidden type, the money that flowed in and out of his hands, the fame, the hangers-on that fed the actor's fragile ego, the adulation of an up and coming movie star, all fueled by vanity of unchecked ambition. He was, however, unlike the so-called "struggling actor." He had solid credentials, and had already established a track record that gave him access to the movers and shakers in this industry, too glad to welcome one with manifest potential. His **résumé** was enviable. Upon his arrival in California he settled at first in an apartment at Alta Loma Terrace, then bought himself a house, drove two cars and gained access to the finest. Why not? To paraphrase his mentor John Houseman, *"he made his money the old fashioned way . . . he earned it."* To say to someone, "you've gone Hollywood" is not exactly a pejorative but a term that may nevertheless lead to conjecture. In Franklyn's case, he had acquired this "noblesse oblige" allure, a condescending flair that others may have called arrogance in his demeanor after flying back to Brooklyn for a brief visit. The tone of his voice had perceptively changed, reminiscent of a character he played on stage. He was definitely no longer the Franklyn we knew. We wondered if the actor in him was permanently set on the ON mode or perhaps he felt so trapped in this dimension that he forgot he was talking to family. Or most likely he knew what he was doing, purposely guarding his privacy, and leaving us scratching our heads. He didn't bunk at his mother's home, finding her no doubt too provincial, preferring instead to be with friends in Manhattan. We caught up with him long enough to query him about life in the rarified air he was breathing in Hollywood. He was somewhat gracious and as usual in a hurry to part company. I could at least claim I shook hands with a celebrity.

During his visit to New York, in-between gigs, Franklyn called his brother Reggie from the Manhattan apartment of a friend he was visiting, inviting him to a party taking place at a penthouse on the West side belonging to some people he knew well, engaged in the theater world.

> "*Reg, I want you to join me. We're going to a party tonight.*
>
> Where are we going?
>
> *Never mind where, just come and meet me at this address . . .* (vintage Franklyn)

"I hurriedly got dressed and headed for the bus to the subway station for the train that would take me to Franklyn's address I wrote on a scrap of paper. Within the hour I met Franklyn dressed in his casuals. We walked a few blocks to our destination. I asked where exactly we were going. '*My agent told me I was invited to a party at a big producer's penthouse.*' A very opulent looking building

I learned after had earned landmark designation. The doorman greeted us. Franklyn immediately volunteered his name. *"Oh yes Mr. Seales, you are expected. Take the elevator to the 36th floor penthouse sir."* The elevator doors open and we notice the rich carved, well-polished wood panels that no doubt date back to several generations.

We enter into a smoke-filled spacious and finely decorated penthouse with a heavy scent of perfumed air of people milling around. Franklyn is greeted by his host with a hug and kisses on both cheeks as the Europeans do. He is wearing a flannel grey pants, an oversized silk white shirt complemented with a light blue dickie around his neck. A very expansive looking man puffing on what looks like a Cohiba Cuban cigar, surrounded by an entourage, I suspect, people he works with in the theater world and now congratulating Franklyn for the completion of his latest project, "The Onion Field" the first film he had shot in Hollywood, being shown now in theaters around the country. So, that's what a big wheel of the theater looks like, I muse. I feel totally lost except when Franklyn points to me and introduces me to his guests, *"This is my brother,"* I hear him say. I'm thinking, I'm totally out of place hanging around with a bunch of white people, some dressed in skin-tight provocative clothing with their faces heavily plastered with makeup, greeting each other with a light touch of both cheeks. Here I'm describing the men . . . I don't know what to say. They speak a different kind of language. I'm only an undergraduate student from the Caribbean trying to be cool. There are some fine looking chicks there as well. My eyes catch one across an oversized table laden with a variety of finger foods manned by two waiters in their crisp white uniforms. She is sipping on a glass of champagne. She is tall and slender in a tight fitting silvery colored dress. She wears her shoulder length red hair loosely around high cheekbone porcelain face, luscious lips painted in burgundy red, matching her hair, and light penetrating eyes. I feel caught in the vortex of the energy she projects, but I quickly recapture control of my space, but it's too late, she slithers in my direction. I drop my eyes to the carpeted floor where one's feet sink into, only to hear a voice close by say,

"Hi, I'm Jennifer, what's your name?" I snap my head to see the same girl up close almost against my chest. I gargle an answer that sounds like, "hi, I'm Reggie." The party has just started for me. I lose sight of Franklyn for the time being. Jennifer is just the girl to put me at ease, and I do feel her vibes.

"Stay right there," I hear her say as she walks away, and comes back with another glass of champagne she hands over to me. "Dang" I'm thinking, these women don't play game here.

"Thank you Jennifer . . . what do you do in New York?" I ask.

"I'm an actress and Franklyn and I done some work together since we were students at Juilliard."

"Really? that's terrific." Of course, I'm thinking, I'm surrounded by actors and actresses, and this one is making a move on me.

"We graduated the same year . . . I'll be heading for Hollywood in the next couple of months after I finish the play I'm in now."

The party goes on into the wee hours of the morning feeling drunk by the conversation Jennifer lured me into consensually. Franklyn and I hop finally on the train for our return to Brooklyn. In my pocket is Jennifer's phone number. It's roughly four o'clock in the morning seated next to a big time movie star. By now, one would think he would have some recognition factor with the public. But apparently, this did not enter Franklyn's consciousness until I began to notice two or three passengers pointing discreetly in our direction and whispering to each other. I turned to Franklyn and say, "Hey Franklyn, I think these people are talking about you . . ." To my surprise, Franklyn becomes visibly uncomfortable. He turns to me and says: *"Hey, let's get off the train . . . these people make me nervous."* "Come on man," I say to him, "everything is cool, you're with me . . . we have only two more stops to make it to Utica Ave." I fail to convince him. He convinces me instead and we get off the train at the next station, then he says, "Let's grab a cab." It's rather ironic that a man who spent years to hone his craft would choose anonymity instead of basking in the spotlight of public recognition." I don't understand his psyche neither do I try to.

*   *   *

"Franco," as the patriarch Francis Seales affectionately called him, was a man on an upward trajectory whose childhood dreams had metastasized from the stage to television and now onto the silver screen. He may not have had time for me, his brother-in-law or his sisters but he was keeping a steady correspondence with his our daughter Natasha, we learned much later. She had reached her early teens and like the other cousins of her age group, Uncle Franklyn had become a demigod, someone she proudly discussed with her school friends. For those who had reached that age group, parents had suddenly become "old fashioned," not keeping up with the latest trends of the early 80's. The teen years were a time of discovery for them. Drawing from our West Indian background, we knew our values did not parallel those of the first generation born in America. We found no rationale, however, to abandon what we cherished, so we told Natasha without equivocation what was expected of her. It was a trying period that challenged our patience after discovering that her uncle Franklyn was advising her to "stand" for herself, essentially to defy us. Since my wife (his sister) and I were brought up under the "old school" which calls for discipline in the West Indian household that contrasted with the "laissez faire" approach dating back to Dr. Spock's teaching, I decided to drop him a letter, measuring my words not to betray my annoyance, but communicating a clear message that we were disapproving his interference, and to inform him in no uncertain terms that his good intentions were not welcomed. Movie star or not, we called the shots in our house. I read him the Riot Act: we knew better how to raise a child, and where did he come off giving parental advice? Franklyn got the message.

In September 1979, Lennox and his wife welcomed their first child, a girl they named Liane. Three months later their little girl underwent corrective heart surgery. They were devastated. His wife and her family were natives of Savannah, GA, and they had spoken many times of leaving New York to start life anew in the city of her birth. He shared his plans with Franklyn whose response was not encouraging:

> *"Why are you moving to the South for? I can hear the derision in his voice, asking me that question.*
>
> *He adds, "You have Karma, Mike, to expand the family."*
>
> *Sorry Franklyn, Juanita and I have discussed this for a long time. We think we made the right decision, I answered.*
>
> *"Who do you know in Georgia? We have no family there . . . Look . . . I will help you . . . I will send your children to college . . ." he countered.*
>
> *"No thanks, Franklyn."*
>
> *"What are you doing? Our father is here . . . Ma is here. Your sisters are here. I'm here. Your uncles are here. The whole family is here, Mike. What are you running from?"*
>
> *"What are you talking about! I'm not running from anything . . . we thought of building a new life for our*

family. We'll come visit, and you'll be invited to visit us, too."

"Franklyn's argument had some merit, and his offer of paying for the children's college education was very tempting but fell on deaf ears." He and Juanita had made a firm decision to leave New York, so June 1980, they packed some of their belongings into the car and headed south, never to look back.

By 1982 Franklyn, assured of his growing success in the industry, buoyed by the knowledge that his fame preceded him, decided to take a trip to his native land. His movie "The Onion Field" released three years earlier in 1979, was shown at the Russell Cinema, one of two theaters on their island paradise. The natives could not contain their exuberance once they recognized one of their own on the screen. Little Franklyn they grew up with in Calliaqua made it to Hollywood and the movies. Sounds unreal at the sound of it. "Impossible" said the skeptics. Leslie, Velma, Barney, Mary and Shaggy, the old gang, gathered in the theater to see if the boy they indeed knew who was so ensconced in his own world had really become a Hollywood celebrity. Sure enough, there he was on the huge screen, the Franklyn, now larger than life, they grew up with, the one who was so full of himself yet drew the admiration of the girls. "Amazing" was the unanimous verdict pronounced, with a mixture of pride and envy. The person who was most taken by this event was Franklyn's ever-loving childhood nanny, Lessie, who had never set foot into the movie theater in her 60+ years of life, was ushered in to see her boy. It was reported that in one of the scenes when the police captures the character, Jessie Youngblood, played by Franklyn and roughed him up, Lessie yelled, *"stop . . . they're killing him . . . they're killing Franklyn . . . stop . . . stop!!!"* Tears streamed from her eyes as she saw her boy being pummeled by law enforcements dragging him inside their squad car. Lessie became inconsolable, grief-stricken. But finally she was once again reunited with her boy who was now a grown man of 30. She was proud of her "son" and spoke to everyone about how she, single handedly-a little exaggeration she figured she could get away with, but quite forgivable-helped bring him into the world and how she cared for him to become the lovable man that he was.

Franklyn took full advantage of his visit in his native land, returning like a conquering hero, drawing the admiration of everyone and everywhere he went and, being the consummate actor that he was, accorded time to share his experiences with eager audiences. He sought out his old neighborhood to visit with Lessie, the opportunity to ask for her forgiveness for the heartaches he caused and to thank her profoundly for the care and devotion to the Seales family. He met the old gang with hugs and kisses; Velma, Leslie, Mary, Barney and "Shaggy." Velma was now married and the mother of four. She was the first to break the awkward silence while they surrounded him in awe of this man, the actor he had predicted he would one day become but whose wild dreams were greeted with skepticism, some even saying that he was "nuts," and going nowhere; but who was laughing now?

"Franklyn, so good to see you again . . ."

"Good to see you too Velma . . . Mary, how are you? Leslie . . . Barney . . . Shaggy . . . great to see you guys."

"Great to see you Franklyn . . ." Mary says . . . "Yeah . . ." echo Barney and Shaggy.

"What are you guys doing?"

"I took over my father's boat" says Barney. "He died a couple years ago. Now I'm doing what he used to do."

"Good for you Barney."

"What about you guys"

"Me and Leslie work for cable and wireless." says Shaggy. "We're doing alright."

"Tell you guys, I'm going to be here for a few days so we'll get together on the beach at Indian Bay for old time sake, how about it?"

"It's a deal," says Leslie who had remained quiet thus far, taking time to reconcile the man with the boy he grew up with and the odd ways he recalls him dreaming about life. There is nothing "odd" about him now.

He stayed at the Minors family who last saw him fourteen years ago since he left the island, arriving two weeks before Christmas. As fate would have it, his guests who were practicing Catholics, invited him to attend church for the tradition of "Nine Mornings," observed the nine days preceding Christmas. During the solemn celebration, one morning a bird flew inside the church, which was not uncommon, and flapped its wings from one end to the other which attracted everyone's attention with the exception of the minister who continued to deliver his homily. At one point, however, the bird briefly circled above Franklyn's head before flying out. This experience seemed at the time rather insignificant yet odd but quickly deemed irrelevant if not rather amusing until years later in 1992 during the service held for the passing of our father, Francis Adolphus Seales, a bird reappeared causing raised eyebrows. Many wondered if it signified Franklyn's return among us.

Franklyn had disapproved his brother's decision to move down South, keenly aware that they were of different minds and pursuing different goals. Lennox never thought that a day would come when Franklyn would want to visit, recalling the disparaging comments he made about his departure and quoting the, shall we say, negative racial history of this section of the country. However after he moved to California and his appearances on television were burgeoning, he would call and write his brother letters disclosing his interest in paying them a visit. He was more than shocked. Sure enough, Franklyn in January 1984 showed up in Savannah. By this time they had an addition to the family, a son they named Gabriel who was then three months old. His affection for Liane and Gabriel was very much in evidence. He was acting very sociable and relaxed with them. He would get down on the floor and play with the kids. He never traveled without his faithful camera, so he was constantly snapping pictures recording his visit. His stay was brief, and they parted company after five days. Lennox was floored once again when Franklyn disclosed that he planned to come for another visit. True to his word, he came back in the spring of 1986.

By this time, Franklyn was in a different realm. He was on television and gaining much notoriety. His name had entered the public domain. Lennox and his wife had moved to another larger home with many amenities that they enjoyed. They were living the American dream. However, upon his arrival, Lennox was subjected to more of his unpleasantness:

"Why live in the suburb while you could have bought a house in the historic district of town?" He asked condescendingly.

"Juanita and I left Brooklyn to escape the urban life that was choking us. Here we have the space we like," I replied.

"Why not? You have these beautiful homes in town . . . you're lucky you married Juanita, without her, you wouldn't be where you are," he sarcastically injected.

"This last comment felt like a hot iron rod poking me in the eye. He got under my skin with those words, giving my wife all the credit. He knew he had said something awkward, but he was determined not to give a damn about my feelings and how he tread on my space. I was happy living in Savannah, yet he couldn't see it. We both worked for the State, she as an educator and I as a mental health counselor. I was living a charmed life and did not need nor could care less about Franklyn's validation.

Franklyn had reached a phase in his career when he was making a sizable sum of "pocket change" to put it in the vernacular, that came with his incremental success, so he behaved and believed what he was saying would hold sway with his brother, predicated by the size of his wallet, which admittedly was considerably larger than his.

"It is truly astonishing how the same childhood arguments, the same dialectic, same ad hominem would suddenly erupt and continue between us within the four walls of MY own home, MY own inviolable castle. His performance shoved in my face, within MY four walls, reinforced my resolve to meet his challenge head on. How audacious, I thought. I'm a thirty eight-year old married man being lectured by the unmarried Franklyn at thirty four in my own living room. Crazy or hard to believe as it may sound, I knew he would not compromise, but I also knew then that I was the one in charge, so speaking with him using words with more than one syllable aroused his suspicion and hardened his stance, but I didn't care. He was not married, but there he was giving me advice on marriage. How dare he! He had no children, yet he believed he could give me a course on child rearing. Crazy! The fact of the matter was, he knew squat. I could discern his insatiable compulsion to be right, to dominate our conversation. With the benefit of hindsight, it was both infuriating and funny as hell."

Gabe, being a very active little boy, was running and pulling away from me at the beach. Franklyn would caution me, "Come on Mike, let the boy run!" That was all cute, but as a parent, I know how quickly the water currents change at the beach in Savannah versus St. Vincent, where there's no rip tide. On these shores, in a blink of an eye, you are lost and gone for good, swallowed by the sea, but he would stubbornly disagree with me. I would observe Gabe running into the sea fully clothed at two years of age. In Franklyn's mind it was okay. "Let him have his freedom," he would insist, rolling his eyes and shrugging his shoulders. All I could envisage was me going to jail for endangering the life of my child. I was the parent and had the parental instinct, yet he would say, "Mike you are acting like Ma; let the child run around and have fun," annoyingly reminding me that I was too protective and proceeding to project into me all of the feelings that he held against Ma for being an overly protective parent. I was confronting a disquieting state of affairs. As hard as I tried, I could not construct an adequate defense triggered by his inflexible intent on telling me what he thought I was doing wrong. Well, it was not about "having fun" as much as it was about being parental and responsible. He had good ideas, but I had to be accountable. I'm also reminded that facts and intelligence often don't beat out the tried and tested 'truth', granted that other points of view have merit. He had intelligence, but you cannot will yourself into a parental mindset-an intellectual exercise I would engage myself to justify my defense-the unthinking celebration of his personal achievements had skewed the kinship I once cherished growing up. My job was to be a parent first. If Gabe was taken by a wave or rip tide, I could not see myself explaining to my wife or the police what I did or didn't do.

We also went on the shores of the Savannah river, a much calmer body of water, a couple of times and once again he engaged me feigning righteous indignation: "let him play." As a responsible parent, I reminded Franklyn how nervous he would make our mother. "Your tactics would not work with me," I told him. I, nonetheless, had to assume a defensive posture, not only as a husband, as a father, but in every aspect of my parental skills. In the end I would be pissed and hoped that he would never come for a return visit. I concluded that the tone can start to be hurtful, attitudes harden, hands are thrown up and the result can be anger or a sense of what's the use he tone can start to be hurtful, attitudes can harden, hands can be thrown up, and the result can be anger or a sense of what's the use? However, much to my disbelief, he, upon his return to California, would call me up to say, "Mike, I gotta tell you that I had a great time with you, Juanita and the kids. You're doing a great job." Go figure . . .

There came a time beginning in 1979 to the late 80's, that Lennox could no longer speak with Franklyn much about his faith or anything of a spiritual nature. He was fiercely against anything he had to share following a statement he wrote in a letter when they first moved to Savannah. "Michael" he began, "you turn to a phantom God because you think your child will die . . . all you're thinking is real estate and yet want to talk to me about God."

In Franklyn's mind, his brother was turning to religion as a matter of convenience not born out of sincere convictions, but because he had had a child who was very sick. Be as it may, he saw things from his own prism. His child was sick. He was strong and stood by his child and things worked out. In the letter he implied that he had a connection to God and that God pulled them out from that place. His response was hurtful, not what he expected,

> *"You're a hypocrite Mike. You've become very materialistic. You're busy buying houses and yet you have the audacity to speak to me about God . . ."*
>
> *He discredits me for being materialistic . . . Funny . . . he went on to buy a home around the same time, as well. I'd called him to congratulate him on his acquisition of the new digs.*
>
> *"Hey Mike" he boasted, "my pool is full of girls."*

He believed that my "phantom God" existed in my limited, narrow, unproductive imagination. Of course, we went ahead and fought about this type of nonsense again and again. I saw this not so much as a spiritual impasse, but more or less Franklyn's irresistible impulse to be right. In every letter, nonetheless, he was expressing his desire to come and visit us, or he was asking for forgiveness for being "out of control" of his quirky behavior; expressing his thoughts "too aggressively" and with such wanton randomness. He "missed" Liane and expressed his desire to come see her. He was a complex man to pin down.

There clearly was a distinct dichotomy between Franklyn the altar boy in St. Vincent, so pious, so attentive to church teachings, so angelic in his devotion, and the Franklyn that talked about the "phantom God" that made absolutely no sense.

> "Mike . . ." he would insist on reminding me, "we are no longer living life on the Island, we are part of the greater world now . . ."

In so many ways he became a wholly different individual who put blinders on to zero in on his burgeoning ego, an essential tool. His personal achievements blurred his reality and those he knew within the family. He would remain fixated on his own philosophy about God and religion; albeit never firmly disclosed to anyone. He would say,

> *"You are looking up to a place named Heaven where there is a white man with a big belly and a beard," representing my "phantom God" that I fantasized, building castles in the air. How degenerative and morally destructive his experience in Hollywood had progressed, I wondered."*

By 1981, Franklyn appeared in Southern Comfort, his second motion picture in two years, teamed with two established movie stars in their own right: Powers Booth and Keith Carradine. Franklyn spoke to his brother about the shooting of this movie in the Louisiana swamps, "cold and damp and fighting mosquitoes." This was undoubtedly the unglamorous side of movie making. In any event, Franklyn's star continued its ascent.

After shooting the movie Southern Comfort, Franklyn returned to California. He called his brother one day and said, "You know, Mike, I suspect I contracted a bug of some kind, a bacterial infection from swallowing that swamp water." He was immediately hospitalized after it was discovered that he had swollen lymph nodes. His doctor proposed the removal of the glands but after a biopsy was conducted, he found the good fortune to learn that no malignancy was discovered. He insisted, however, on his brother telling no one in the family, a request he kept but made him wonder why the secrecy. What did he have to hide from the family? His request added more stress to their turbulent relationship but one "secret" that he had no intention of betraying. It became a waiting game. He gave him no reason to believe he would not recover from a benign surgery.

More acclaims would come to Franklyn when he was cast in the American sitcom, "Silver Spoons," which featured the main character, young Ricky Schroeder. He played the role of Dexter Stuffins, the erudite uncle of break dancing nephew Alfonso Spears featuring a very talented young actor, Alfonso Ribeiro. Between 1983 and 1987, Franklyn became a fixture on that show brought to us every week into our living rooms in living color. The cast of the show became his primary family, brought on by the constant interaction with his colleagues that was not limited to production time but extended to invitations to the homes of his co-stars. We learned he was a frequent visitor at Ricky Schroeder's house to partake in his mother's home cooking. In addition to Silver Spoons, he was also featured in an episode of the sitcom AMEN in which he appeared with a very special guest, a mega star in the Pop music world, the one and only, the renown Whitney Huston. She was Franklyn's love interest in a scene when the two are shown in a passionate, soulful kiss that left nothing to the imagination. When their lips finally parted after the seconds ticked away, Whitney lowered her face and let out an audible erotic sound signaling Franklyn had hit her erogenous zone. His expression however was one that characterized the mindset of a man exhibiting supreme confidence in his charm. He kept his head slightly tilted upward while giving Whitney a subtle grin that said, "I have conquered you, my Diva." From that faint head fake we could discern the consummate Calliaqua native son, Franklyn Vincent Ellison Seales. The scene with Whitney "the Diva," however, was not the fluid kiss the viewers saw on their screen, Franklyn explained, "it took us nearly 30 takes to get it right," he said. "What happened . . . I mean, why did it take so many takes?" I asked. "She was a bit nervous and that made me feel uncomfortable, so the director had us do it over and over until he was satisfied . . . remember she isn't a trained actress and he didn't think we could just wing it . . . hey, I didn't mind kissing her for as long as it took . . . how many guys can say they kissed Whitney Huston, huh?" "You got that right bro . . ." My response could not disguise a hint of envy registering in my voice.

Christmas 1986, in the midst of his busy schedule, Franklyn found time to fly to New York to spend Christmas with the family. As was the custom we observed for several years, we had gathered at my house and his family's house. Between the Dorsinvilles, the Seales and the Richardsons, consisting of grandparents, parents, in-laws, several nephews and nieces, and one three-week-old niece, we had a nice crowd pregnant with anticipation of Franklyn's arrival. I had my video camera set on ready to record the grand entrance with his entourage. He didn't disappoint any of us. As he walked into the room displaying a certain panache, he immediately spotted the camera and with mocked shyness shielded his face with a box bearing a Christmas gift. He flashed a huge smile, sporting a California tan, sans makeup, wearing a grey jacket with matching pants and shirt, a scarf around his neck with one end flung across his left shoulder à la Hollywood style. A flow of excitement filled the room in an instance, everyone rushing to get a close up of him and to hear the stories we all wanted to know about his world of make believe.

"How is everybody?" he shouted with a broad smile.

The ladies were the first recipients of hugs and kisses he gladly exchanges. We observed him absorbing the adulation he had grown accustomed to receiving from his peers on the West Coast. Coming from members of the family must be icing on the cake. He didn't take time to reach for the latest member of the family, three-week-old Ashley. He spoke without pause, content to perform before an audience that gave him their undivided attention.

Franklyn's world continued to expand. We heard he was travelling to Italy accompanied by some friends. In December of 1987, Lennox and his family drove to Brooklyn to celebrate Christmas together with his mother, his sisters Joy, and Leslie, and their respective families. Franklyn flew in from California. He had quite unexpectedly lowered his guards and laid aside his weapons. We found him extremely personable and jovial, unlike other times when the two brothers kept each other's company that invariably deteriorated into silly arguments. And his decision to stay at the house in Brooklyn this time totally immersed in our culture heightened suspicions of his underlying motives. This was totally out of character for him to stay at the house. Far be it for us to query his motives. The youngest brother, Regis, was getting married early January 1988. Franklyn decided, again to our astonishment, to remain in Brooklyn for the celebration. To the untrained eyes he looked like he had lost some body weight, yet he gave us no warning that he was slowing down. He was still functioning well. He had good energy. The morning came, bringing us closer to the hour of the event, and we were dressing up when Franklyn asked his brother to help him put on his tie. At this point, he noticed how bony his neck looked; he had lost muscle mass in his neck and shoulders, which he found quite odd, but dismissed without drawing his attention, preferring to believe that he was probably following a Hollywood fad diet in preparation for a role. As hard as he tried to answer his own questions, *"I felt like I was digging a hole and with each shovel, the mystery grew deeper. I felt like I had picked up on something. What was that 'something?' I didn't know. I felt a vague uneasiness notwithstanding his nonchalant demeanor. At the reception I observed how happy he looked dancing with all the women in attendance and how much at ease he put everyone. It looks like he was unknowingly upstaging the groom with his antics that were nonetheless well received by the family."*

"At the time of these new developments, I was working in a hospital with access to doctors from various disciplines. I asked an oncologist what Franklyn's symptoms-drawn solely on my subjective observations—indicated. His answer was painfully direct: 'I suspect your brother may be positive for HIV/AIDS. Of course you understand, I'm guessing Mike, and basing it solely on the symptoms you reported to me that narrow the diagnosis.' His words came as an unexpected shock. Hearing this doctor's verdict, I wondered if Franklyn knew of his fate and was putting on his final act."

After the wedding, he flew to Canada for the filming of an episode for the TV show "Wise Guys." Days later, seated at home in Savannah looking at the telecast, Lennox suddenly felt an indefinable pressure that sent his head throbbing in pain, a sense of dread overtaking him, while mysteriously whispering, "Franklyn is sick . . ." He spent the night in an out of sleep, his mind in a turmoil, unable to slow down his out of control thought patterns. His wife detected his restlessness and asked, "What's wrong, Mike?" "Nothing." he answered. She went back to sleep. As daylight approached, he felt an urgent compulsion to write him a letter expressing his concerns and seeking an answer to this nagging question that had taken residence in his consciousness. Within a week he received a call and heard a voice telling him,

"Are you sitting down Mike?"

I immediately felt a heavy load crashing down on my shoulders while losing all sense of time and space. His question sounded too ominous and threatening, which only served to deepen my feeling of helplessness.

"Yeah, I am," I answered with heavy trepidation,

"What's up Franklyn?" I asked. My voice cracked in a futile attempt to deflect the words that would confirm my suspicions.

"Mike," he said, "I'm HIV positive," echoing the doctor's diagnosis I had heard a few weeks before. I felt the blood draining out of my body followed by tingling electrical impulses running up and down the surface of my skin, gripped by a stiffness in my neck triggering throbbing pain radiating down my spine. I concluded at that precise moment that my brother Franklyn was handed a death sentence and had finally communicated his helplessness to me. A swelling in my throat precluded an immediate answer. He sensed my silence and the heaviness in my breathing.

"I'll be alright Mike . . ." he said, his voice sounding upbeat, the tone he served to camouflage the illness that had begun to ravage his body, while trying to assuage my worst fear.

"I know some good people in Mexico and in Italy who treat people like me . . . there's hope, Mike."

My senses felt numb for a few hours that stretched into days as I tried to find solace in this sea of despair, trusting or hoping that he was no doubt wrong, the doctors were wrong, the diagnosis was wrong. I shared the news with my wife. Franklyn then called his sisters Joy, Pat and Leslie, the latter immediately breaking down into tears. All of the color ran from her face as she collapsed onto the chair, head in hands, visibly shaken. She recalls Franklyn telling her, "Don't cry Les, I'll be alright . . ." She went to a place where she could not find her way out. It was one of the most powerful revelations to befall our family that left us all in a state of suspended animation.

Crossroads and final encounters are areas where human resolve is most severely tested. When and if we pass through them, we can never be the same again. It was pure terror that visited us in those moments. So back in 1981, he and his doctor had no clue. Diagnosis of this condition was in its infancy, and treatment was still years in the distant future. However, his swollen lymph glands was the first sign that he was infected, though he looked deceptively well and took care of himself. Yet a shadow remained hanging over him, and only a matter of time separated the progression of his illness before it surfaced in full force.

Well, when I first saw him in Savannah in January 1984, he lay low, subdued, remaining in neutral. I observed him gulping several vitamin pills. On his second visit in 1986 he was losing muscle and looked unmistakably smaller. All of these signs gave us pause but were no absolute indicators that Franklyn had reached the apex of life's journey and had begun to slide back on that steep slope, slowly at first, gathering speed each year, over months, followed by weeks; each lap pointing to the inevitable certainty.

So, his trip to Italy was not for some R and R as I thought. He went there to seek a possible cure for his illness, some sort of a silver bullet that would reverse the progressive deterioration of his body, this mysterious illness that had the medical profession on full alert. It finally made sense. Our brother was in a full panic mode that he cleverly concealed from all of us. I prodded him for a clue, but my questions were met with stubborn rejections.

THE RETURN

In the beginning of 1989, Franklyn's illness had progressed beyond the point of deniability; hence, he could no longer function at the level his profession demanded of him and that defined his very existence. It was a goal he pursued with reckless abandon that became his raison d'être, for which he had dedicated his entire life. There was a notable difference in his dance: phone conversations took a dramatic and puzzling turn, centered more on gratitude and blessings rather than being confrontational. At one point in a phone conversation, he revealed that he was contemplating the sale of his house.

> *"Hear this, Franklin, sell the house and move to Savannah where you can buy a very nice house on the beach," I aggressively suggested.*
>
> *"No Mike, I'll buy me a loft where I can do my painting and also do community theatre right here in this city," stubbornly dismissing my suggestion.*
>
> *"Come to Savannah, Franklyn. We'll take you in," begging him to let go of his foolish pride and to say simply: "yes" or "I'll think it over."*

He declined.

By late 1989, I received an unexpected but welcomed call informing me that after an exhaustive review of his finances, he was moving out of the loft. He had finally concluded that he was spending more money than he was bringing in. He was in the midst of packing most everything and shipping it to me. He mentioned rugs, a huge sofa and other personal items. He also had his prized Ford Mustang transported across country to my house.

One is again reminded of the words of T.S. Eliot *"We shall not cease from exploration and the end of all our exploring will be to arrive where we started and know the place for the first time."* Franklyn had explored the very depth of his being, had found his calling and followed every path, every spring of water, every hill, every mountain crest, only to return to the valley that revealed from whence he came. He returned to his beginning, rediscovering the past he had renounced with a hunger that craved fulfillment. Like the prodigal son returning to his father, he was reliving and acknowledging the culture, the family that gave him birth and nurtured his dreams. He realigned himself with his inner self. He reentered every room and turned on all the lights and saw his relationship with us and begged for reconciliation. He requested all the indigenous foods that he had shunned, now coated with a discerned humility that heretofore was anathema to the persona he had cultivated in his pursuit for temporal fame. Mindful of this transitory life, he asked to return to Calliaqua, but his brother discouraged him. He'd heard the incident of his sister taking him to the movies and in the middle of the performance him becoming violently sick, regurgitating on the floor. Flying for five hours was too much of a challenge.

My wife, Leslie and I had a long phone conversation with Franklyn:

Fall of 1989, the phone rings in the early evening hours. I hear Leslie's voice engaged in a conversation but can only hear her say, "yes" . . . "no" . . . "when?" . . . I watch her listening intently as she drifts away to the adjacent room. She returns and hands me the receiver and whispers "Franklyn." I barely recognize the now flattened voice by:

"Hi Jean . . . I want to return home . . . and I would like to stay a few days at your house with you and Leslie, and Dimitri . . . would that be okay?" I hear him say hesitantly.

"Sure . . . of course Franklyn, what's up?"

"I'll let you know . . . when I plan to leave L.A. for New York."

"That's fine Franklyn; just let us know when you plan to arrive."

"I will . . . thanks, Jean."

I hear a click and turn to Leslie and the empty look in her eyes says she is also without a clue. She proceeds to call her mother who expressed her puzzlement and was also unable to fill in the gaps. She follows with a call to her brother in Savannah who gave us the rundown on what was quickly unfolding. We were living in Somerset, N.J. at the time with our son Dimitri. Our daughter Natasha was attending Howard University in Washington DC. We then learned that he had sold his house and much of his furniture. He had his car transported to Savannah for his brother Lennox; at the same time he sent us an antique armoire and several of his paintings that were eventually given to his youngest sister. I also learned of a rumor that lent much credibility to our suspicions. In Franklyn's progressive debilitating state, unbeknown to us at the time, his heath had become more perilous by the day. His focus was waning, impairing his decision process. A coin collection and other personal items he mentioned to us never made it to Somerset. We, however, received empty containers in which he stored these coins. The parasitic vultures that surrounded him during his most vulnerable hours feasted on his belongings that were destined for the family in Brooklyn.

Leslie and I and her brother Reggie proceeded to JFK located at a distance of fifty miles one way from our house to welcome him on a cool and breezy late September afternoon. I wondered how his already weakened body would react to the change of climate. As he entered the passenger arrival area, we were taken aback by the unexpected appearance of the man precariously ambling in our direction. He had already become a shadow of himself. He had dropped an easily perceivable amount of weight. His clothes swallowed his frail body. Where flesh once filled his cheeks was now melted. His skin was pulled tightly against the cheek bones. His lips barely met, exposing his teeth giving him the appearance of a frozen smile. His eyes had sunk deeper into their sockets. He walked slowly toward us, each step straining against the weight of his backpack which I quickly retrieved from him. Alas, he was no longer the pugnacious Franklyn we knew and verbally thrust and parried with. I quickly surmised we had a challenging task on our hands that we were ill-prepared to undertake. Nonetheless, for the next three weeks, Leslie and I went on a mission to assist Franklyn who was in the battle of his life and we were praying for a hopeful recovery. Leslie fed him with the proper nutrients that would help rebuild his depleted body and remained at his side catering to his needs to ease the hours passing by. Though mindful of his condition and the controversial mystery surrounding the transmission of this deadly disease, we were convinced that our exposure would not alter our way of life. He had his own bedroom and shared the same bathroom with our son. He ate in the same plates and utensils we used. We embraced both him and his tormentor. This said, we had this nagging thought about how this disease was transmitted. The literature at the time was not very reassuring and we were reminded of the precaution we should take when Leslie received a call from her sister who sounded more alarmed than we were. "*Don't forget to clean his plates with very hot water . . . and use Lysol spray everywhere,*" she advised Leslie. One day, I drove him to his doctor for a scheduled visit at the hospital in Manhattan. An hour went by for whatever was needed done that included giving a urine specimen and three vials of blood. As he came out of the office, we got on the elevator and Franklyn turned to me, visibly shaken, his face at a foot distance of mine expressing his concerns. I felt his saliva landing on my cheek that I quickly wiped, and a sense of dread settling that I concealed from him.

*   *   *

Reggie confirmed my impression when he shared his thoughts with me: *"I almost did not recognize him. He looked much older, frail and sick. I was looking at a man who had deteriorated considerably since I saw him about one year ago! I felt sorry for him and did not want to believe what I was looking at. But we both kept our composure and greeted him as normally as the conditions allowed. The ride home to Brooklyn was quiet by our standards; our conversation was measured and we did not discuss his physical condition. We both held it together well and did not show how overwhelmed/shocked we were to see Franklyn in such a physically compromised condition. Sadly this was the beginning of the end for Franklyn and we were on our way to confronting the inevitable."*

He had finally distanced himself from the land of make believe for now. The change of environment suited him and could not have arrived a day sooner. He had time to rest while emptying his mind of the high pressure world he abandoned that entrapped him, and now threatened his very existence. He was sunning himself every day on the deck. Day after day, we began to notice a perceived rejuvenation. His growing appetite surely became a good indicator of the inner healing taking place. There was an obvious weight gain that brought us a degree of relief coupled with his old fighting spirit that became more noticeable day after day. He walked with greater assurance and flair, signaling that his health was ameliorating; all in combination brought him surcease from the urgency that we saw when he first arrived. Several of his friends from California and Manhattan who called the house to speak to him were solicitous and offered encouragement. In answer to their questions, he would often say, *"My sister Leslie is an angel . . . she is taking good care of me."* We frequently took him to the supermarket with us and introduced him to the city of Somerset we now called home since leaving Brooklyn the year before. He enjoyed the tranquility, the serenity around him, the trees that reminded him of his childhood days in Calliaqua. We began to believe that the worst was over and began to entertain the thought of a miraculous cure. Yes, hope springs eternal. It is salubrious.

Franklyn's younger brother Reggie was also a resident of New Jersey who lived in Princeton about a half hour drive from our house in Somerset. One day, sometime in October, I received a call from Reggie whose tone of voice sounded very upbeat at the end of the line.

"Jean" he said, "I went to an October Fest in Lawrenceville where I met the owners of an art gallery."

"Ok, what's going on, Reg?" I inquired.

"I went in this art gallery that displayed and sold a variety of paintings from mostly local artists, I was told. At one point I approached the owner and introduced myself to him:

"Sir, my name is Reggie. I've been admiring your paintings."

"Great, which ones do you like?"

"I like all of them," I said, "but I want to tell you about an artist who happens to be a known actor of screen and television. His name is Franklyn Seales, my brother."

"Oh, interesting, tell me more. What movie was he in?"

"The one you might have seen him is called 'The Onion Field.'"

"Sure, I saw that movie with James Woods. You mean the other character is your brother? Cool"

"He also was a regular in a television series called, Silver Spoons."

"Yeah . . . with . . . what's his name again?"

"Ricky Schroeder, you're thinking . . ."

"Yeah, yeah, that's him."

"Well, you see sir, besides his acting, he is also a painter and is now exploring the possibility of selling some of his work. I think you might be interested in looking at this work."

"At this point the owner is looking at me in disbelief. I continue to tell him that the art is stored in the basement of your house in Somerset. He continues to give me a skeptical look but I ask him if he would be interested to come to the house and look at the collection."

"I sure am. When can I see his work. I'm available next Sunday afternoon . . ."

"I'm sure I can arrange that with my sister where the paintings are stored. I'll give you a call to give you the direction."

That's great news, Reg, Here, I'll put on Franklyn, and you can tell him yourself.

To my surprise, going by Franklyn's answers and tone of his voice, perhaps not wanting to get his expectations too high, he at first, sounded very skeptical, asking, "Who is this guy Reggie?" He finally relents and tells Reggie to bring the gentleman to the house to view the collection. The following weekend, Reggie, accompanied by the gallery owner arrives at the house, hoping, as Reggie puts it, "to blow his mind with the positive surprise he was going to hit him with." Leslie, Franklyn and I give him a warm welcome and invites him to the basement where the paintings are stored. After some initial quiet and somewhat tense moments it was clear that the gallery owner was simply blown away by Franklyn's eclectic style of modern art. From his reaction and body language it was clear that he never expected to find such a variety of refined modern art painted by a prolific young painter and accomplished actor in a basement in Somerset NJ. The art gallery owner complimented Franklyn and had nothing but praise for his work. In short order they drafted a working contract and subsequently agreed to the terms and conditions as applied to selling his works of art.

Franklyn, expectedly, was delighted that his art finally made it into the main stream. From the initiation of the art contract to the time of his death he earned approximately $20,000 from his art sales. What's important here is the gratification Franklyn received knowing that one of his many goals was accomplished when he finally received some commercial recognition for his art. "In a strange way," Reggie recalls, "bringing Franklyn and the art gallery owner together was probably my biggest contribution to his life."

After three weeks with us, Franklyn had regained the spring in his steps and felt well enough to return to his mother's house in Brooklyn. A pyrrhic change."

1990 came without much fanfare. Weeks passed, followed by months during which Franklyn's precarious health status continued to focus the family's attention. He showed remarkable resilience in his recovery's progression. He was able to resume some of his activities. He would travel on the subway to visit friends in Manhattan and carry as normal a life he could will himself. At other times we would find him sequestered in his room sketching and painting enabling him a venue for his unrelenting drive to showcase his creativity.

By April 1990 the news filtered through that he was hospitalized at St. Vincent Hospital in Manhattan. Lennox immediately rescheduled his family obligations and drove up from Savannah, covering the distance in eighteen hours non-stop. he had reached what is clinically referred to as the "wasting syndrome," a condition characterized by weight loss associated with chronic fever and diarrhea. One section in the hospital was designated for Aids patients only. Access to his room required the use of a face mask. As Lennox pulled a chair next to his bed, Franklyn made what he thought was an unusual or should I say a surprise request:

"I want you to wash my hair Mike." I hear him say.

I comply with nary a second thought.

"Now I want you to comb my hair and give me a shave," he adds.

"Now slap me with some cologne, Mike."

"What?" I mused.

"You still have a lot of vanity, Franklyn." I said, half jokingly.

"Mike," I hear him say, "My body is dead but my mind is alive."

"You know Mike . . ." he pauses, "I wish I could do this . . ."

"Do what Franklyn?"

"I want to give my mind to one of your children, Mike."

"What?! How do you plan to do that Franklyn?" Puzzled and at the same time amused by his offer.

"Never mind that! That's what I want to do . . . yes, my body may be dying but my mind is totally alive. I want to give it away."

"I see . . ." unable to complete a full sentence, trying to digest his utterance.

At this juncture of their lives, Lennox and his wife had no interest in adding another mouth to their family: *"We were done with more children. We had the two we wanted, and that was that. The medication is no doubt affecting Franklyn's brain, I suspected, or where in the world did he get this idea?"* He dismissed their conversation and deleted it from memory as he left the hospital hoping to see him discharged during his brief visit.

A day later they received a call informing them that his condition had stabilized and he was ready to be discharged from the hospital. A special bed was delivered to the house. A nurse by the name of Joy who coincidentally bears his sister's name, was assigned to him. She was heaven sent. She had a very charismatic personality that was reflected in her devotion to her patient: very jovial, cheerful, with a genuine awareness of Franklyn's needs. The sentiments were reciprocated. Franklyn was smitten by her devotion and gentle spirit. A doctor visited him to administer medications and to check his condition.

Lennox reflected on Franklyn's long held dialectic tension originating from early childhood, the cycle that exists for every and any living thing, especially a gifted one. Their mother was so humble and so ordinary in his eyes; nonetheless, she always knew that it was youth pitted against wisdom, and in the end she clung to the knowledge that wisdom would prevail. So at times tolerated her intolerant son and internalized his put downs, insensitivity and youthful ignorance. There was mutual love, but Franklyn was also steadfast with his polemics against her though he knew not what he was talking about most of the times when it came to his mother. So, Lennox witnessed this relational dynamic between mother and son for years. The mother, giving in and being supportive, Franklyn fault finding and at times, downright insulting. Old habits die hard. Then, the entire dynamic brought Franklyn back to his mother's humble abode a very sick man. His mother who was not too well herself, was there, still accepting, still loving and still tolerant.

So my brother returned home to Brooklyn, an ill and broken young man. The time had come, I hoped, for Franklyn and Ma to be in touch with a fundamental part of the mother-son relationship that heretofore had been lost, or dare I say may not have ever been present in a long time for Franklyn. There he was, a light once so bright, and now relegated to the darkest place. Our mother was the tower of power, gracefully moving forward, caring and providing a safe loving place for her ailing son. She would embrace the day and do whatever it took to make him comfortable and safer than ever. In the end, Franklyn had a rude awakening as he came to realize the magnitude of the energy and the love that Ma possessed. It was not about her apparent ordinary humility, but the depth of her spirit and unlimited love and capacity to love that moved him. He transitioned into a position of neutrality.

He was there in Brooklyn, distanced from his former life, no longer rebelling against anyone or anything, but manifesting a hunger for all that he once rejected but came to cherish as he lived the last days of his life. He requested that we play West Indian music that shaped his boyhood days. He sojourned back to the food Lessie fed him in Calliaqua: Codfish cakes, rice and peas, Mauby, pigtail soup, sugar cake. His mother and sister Joy took turn preparing his meals. He had curiously developed an insatiable appetite for the culture he once shunned. This hunger for the things that molded his youth came back to him with forceful intent and in limitless abundance bringing him the joy and the innocence of growing up barefoot in the streets of Calliaqua. In the end, Franklyn justly closed the gap, the abyss that had been crafted by circumstances that are better left buried. The younger brother was able to leave this life knowing that he came from a special family. They were giving him a legacy of everlasting love. Their mother was always the one with the deep love despite fighting her own inner battles. It was felt that in Franklyn's last days, he made peace with himself and his God. He came to embrace his family and especially his mother. He died knowing that he was a success by every measure or stretch of the imagination. He had relentlessly pursued a temporal dream, and it was not deferred. He chased that dream like a tiger after prey. He satisfied this primitive hunger that occupied every cell of his body. He came home to Brooklyn to find the last piece . . . the love that was always there waiting, always unconditional and magnanimous.

On his return to Savannah Lennox frequently inquired about his recovery-if it were objectively possible by denying or postponing acceptance of the obvious-and to facilitate their mother's recognition of the inevitable. Days were flashing by very quickly during the month of May; then he began counting the hours, receiving news that were neither encouraging nor dire. He was experiencing severe bouts of diarrhea that further complicated his condition, accelerating the body's inability to muster the strength to mount a winnable defense. The days were never alike. His condition, one day, seemed to be in remission characterized by the demeanor of a man that had regained control of the situation, yet, other days, he could barely get out of bed to face his routine of devoting his time to his canvas for his latest creation or to speak to a friend calling to wish him well. Mother Olive's time was spent in constant surveillance for what we were all resigned to hear.

His final "curtain call" came on May 14, 1990 shortly after the midnight hour amidst sustained thunderous applause from an audience that had grown to celebrate a gifted Shakespearean actor at work. Only after the lights had begun to dim, one by one they filed out of the theater completely enthralled by another brilliant performance . . .

One can only imagine.

Reggie had stayed in touch with Franklyn from the time he had arrived from Los Angeles to the day he died.

"As I recall, Reggie says, *"Ma called me and said he was 'very low' (near death), so I decided to leave work early and go to my mother's house in Brooklyn to see him. He was indeed 'very low' just as she aptly said. He acknowledged my presence and barely gestured hello to me. His frail skeleton—looking body laid practically lifeless on the bed, the scene was overwhelming. He was literally half the man he once was. His immense suffering was about to be rescued by death! Our cousin Sylvanus (Syl) was in the room with us. I do not recall what I said, but the gravity of the situation shook me to my core. I was scared! While talking to Syl, Franklyn somehow summoned the strength to sit-up, Syl said 'you see Reggie, God is good!' Franklyn with a single tear drop rolling out from both eyes said 'I finally accepted*

my mortality . . . I love you all' as Syl helped him to lie down. I held his hand and said good bye to him knowing that this is most probably my last good bye. I left the house in a saddened state, unable to fathom the inevitable fate that awaited him in a matter of hours, if not minutes, but I took solace knowing that his suffering was about to end and he would soon be in a better place. Franklyn died the following day . . ."

May 13, 1990 marked Mothers' Day. Leslie and I drove from our home in New Jersey to Brooklyn to join the family and spend the day with Franklyn who was bedridden and showed no sign of strength to engage in his daily routine of working on a canvas. By then he was receiving around the clock nursing care. His morning nurse remained vigilant in his room throughout the day. We arrived around midday greeted by the voice of the nurse singing the hymn Franklyn loves so much and that rekindled memories of his years as an altar boy,

'Blessed Assurance, Jesus is mine! Oh, what a foretaste of glory divine! Heir of salvation, purchase of God, Born of His Spirit, washed in His blood.'—Franklyn's voice, now a whisper, joins in the chorus,—*This is my story. This is my song . . .*
'Praising . . . my Savior . . . all the daylong; This . . . is my story, this is my song, Praising my Savior all the day long.'

"He is not looking well . . ." Leslie remarks. He looks emaciated, resembling the same man we met at the airport a few months before. His hair had thinned considerably, leaving a few patches on his scalp. His sunken eyes stared fixated on the ceiling and his leathery skin covered very little of flesh that had literally melted, accentuating his skeleton. The nurse remained by his side holding a wet cloth in her hand. She repeatedly wiped his parched lips caused by a low grade fever. He received an injection of morphine to mask the pain that is wracking what is passed as his skeletal body. Summoning the little strength he had he signaled for water in a feeble grunting sound. The nurse holds a cup with a straw to his mouth. He lacks the strength to suck a few drops. She removes the straw and attempts to pour the water into his mouth, but the water drips back out from the corner of his lips that remain open. She crushes a cube of ice, gently rubs a small piece on his lips and inserts it in his mouth. I hear him groan as he tries to shift his body to one side. Each breath becomes more labored. I notice Ma's retreating into her room. She had reached a point where she could no longer witness Franklyn's descent. Joy and I remain by his bed until the nurse indicates her assignment for the day is over at 6:00 PM to be relieved by the night nurse. Before leaving she offers a few words of encouragement to Ma, but we knew that she knew and I suspect that she knew that we knew that death had entered the room several hours before, hovering over his bed. She offered a heartfelt prayer. We decide to leave as well and drive the nurse home. Joy and the night nurse remain by his side but she advises Joy to go to bed. The clock strikes midnight and Franklyn's descent accelerates and the end comes. 'O DEATH, WHERE IS YOUR VICTORY? O

225

DEATH, WHERE IS YOUR STING?' Saint Paul in 1Corinthians reminds us. *'The sting of death is sin, and the power of sin is the law; but thanks be to God, who gives us the victory through our Lord Jesus Christ.'* The nurse enters Joy's room and whispers the news but Ma overhears the steps in the hallway and the chatter . . . Her moans begin and do not end . . . Joy is left to close his eyes.

The applause had faded . . . his stentorian voice permanently silenced . . . like a flickering glow of a candle in the wind, his fire was snuffed out. He was only thirty seven, much too young, one will say for Franklyn to past into the beyond, yet in these condensed years, he had amassed considerable living that may inspire those yearning to reach beyond themselves. His was not a scripted journey drafted by a Hollywood writer, a fantasy world designed to transport the audience to another dimension of the mind, to escape its sometimes troubled world or monotonous existence. His in fact was predestined as the steward of the gifts he was bestowed at birth and from which he made the most. The circumstances leading to his death seemed almost counterintuitive, given his zest for life. To paraphrase the words of Martin Luther King: Like anybody, Franklyn would have liked to live a long life; I would have liked to grow old with him, longevity has its place but he had already been to the mountain pinnacle of Hollywood and scanned the sublime, the dreadful, and the repulsive.

In the early morning of May14, the phone rings. I hear Joy's raspy voice whispering that my beloved brother had drifted off to eternal sleep. I inhale deeply to absorb the shock. I feel the touch of a hand tugging at my pants and turn to his seven year old nephew Gabriel. I mouth the news to him. I immediately see sadness registered on my son's face as the tears well in his eyes. His expression of sorrow was of the purest of innocence without full understanding of the process that ends the life cycle. For a few moments I embrace him as we both shed tears that console each other; then, we immediately sprung into action, leaving my mother-in-law in charge of Liane and Gabriel while Juanita and I made our preparations to attend Franklyn's funeral with family and friends gathered at the funeral parlor in Brooklyn. Word had traveled quite fast among the St Vincent Diaspora living in New York and it was a source of comfort to meet native Vincentians coming to pay their respects to their fellow native son. Following a script he had left with detailed instructions, we had his body cremated and two days later, I and Juanita boarded the Pan Am plane to Barbados where we changed for the LIAT connection to St Vincent to have his ashes scattered at sea, not just anywhere but after his insistence that they should be at a specific point in the ocean we scattered his ashes where one could have a panoramic view of Ratho Mill, Calliaqua, Villa and Indian Bay.

Upon arrival on the Motherland, my first visit was to Lessie in the two-bedroom house I spent my boyhood years with Franklyn, the house that held many cherished memories when life was so simple and predictable. I step into the past, walk on Labourne street practically a stranger. I recognize no one and no one recognizes me, I but am greeted with stares. The old people are dead, my generation migrated to the US and other shores. I hold the urn containing the ashes tightly against my chest as I approach the house now barely standing on moldy wood frames washed by sun and rain. The shade of the mango trees create a refreshing oasis in the yard. I catch a glimpse of her engaged in the same rituals repeated for as long as I can remember, stroking the fire under the same black cast iron pot in which she is cooking her soup du jour. She wears a plaid dress that had endured many cleanings. Her head is wrapped in a perpetual bandana soaked with perspiration. Her large bare feet firmly planted as one with mother earth. My heart quickens as she turns her head over her left shoulder to look in the direction of the steps she hears approaching. Our eyes meet. I stop. For a brief moment I detect her hesitation. She mops beads of sweat dripping into her eyes, looks again more intently and at once her grip on the large spoon loosens and falls mindlessly on the ground, "Michael . . . is that you?" she lets out a scream that shatters the usual serenity of the day, inviting the barking of the dogs roped in the neighbor's yard. Windows fly open and the "newcomer"-me-the native son of a past generation that everyone takes for an intruder falls under the scrutiny of the curious eyes. She rushes toward me. I feel the pressure of two strong arms flung around my neck, pulling me tighter to her while I cautiously maintain a grip on the urn I hold in one hand. I feel my whole body locked in a vise.

"Oh Lawd . . . oh Lawd, that you Michael? my boy . . . my boy . . . it's you Michael, oh Michael."

Her welcome is so joyful, so adoring.

"Where is everybody? I'm so happy to see you . . ."

I can't respond. I grind my teeth, momentarily stricken by a wave of emotions that paralyzes my jaws. It takes me a moment or two to compose myself and not betray the anguish that brings me to her. She looks at me and stares at the urn and says,

"What you got in your hand?"

I rapidly swallow the bulging swelling in my throat and respond,

"Lessie, let's sit down . . . come . . . let's go inside the house."

She follows me in. I pull the old wood chair close to mine, but she remains standing akimbo as I rest the urn on the table. I look at her face but quickly drop my eyes attempting to steady myself for the news I came to deliver to my surrogate mother. I feel the stare of her eyes examining me, my every breath, my uncomfortable and awkward body movements. I reach and take both of her hands in mine and press tightly. Her palms feel rough, moist with nervous perspiration-mixed with mine-and strong from years of manual labor, but I am thrilled holding those precious hands. My dear Lessie is with me once again after more than twenty five years since I left for America. I raise my face to catch the glimpse in her expectant eyes glistening with tears, now befuddled by my almost dramatic appearance at the house and finding herself in an uncompromising position lovingly looking at me, peering downward unknowing of the words I am about to deliver. I clear my throat and say half whispering,

"Lessie . . . I came . . . to bury Franklyn's ashes."

"What!? . . . what did you say?"

I sense her arms trembling, a trembling that travels through her whole body.

"I inhale deeply and am drawn into Lessie's eyes peering intently deep inside of me and I blurt . . . Franklyn is dead."

"No! Nooooooo!" she shrieks. "Franklyn . . . my baby . . . my boy Franklyn!"

Her voice bellows at the top of her lungs as her legs collapse under her body and she crashes in a heap against the hard wooden floor with a thud, sobbing uncontrollably, calling Franklyn's name in a staccato rhythm. Neighbors who heard Lessie's distressing yell, in quick steps, approach the house and peer through the open window whispering and wondering what could have happened to Lessie. For the next half hour I remain by Lessie with her legs crouched tightly against her torso, lying in a fetal position until her body stops convulsing. I pull her to the chair. I sit her down and wipe the tears.

We are introduced to a newly assigned Minister, Father Painter, at the Calliaqua Anglican Church who conducts a solemn service before a gathering of villagers, friends, relatives, onlookers who knew our family well. The service began at nine o'clock in a church packed tight in that hot endless summer climate, a few folding chairs extending beyond the bare wooden pews to capture the overflow, while others stand along the walls, still others outside peering through the open windows ventilating the sweaty air, to pay tribute to this son of Calliaqua. Joining us were his nieces, Natasha and Monique, who by pure coincidence had, months before Franklyn's death, booked their passage for St Vincent, the land of their respective mothers, for a "well-deserved vacation," as they put it. The urn containing Franklyn's ashes is placed on the altar. The minister extends his condolences to the family and delivers a homily that feels like a balm that soothes our sin-sick souls. The service lasts more than one hour with to tributes interspersed by Lessie's loud sobs. Juanita, my brother, Ells, and I are joined by Franklyn's childhood friend to board the boat on a beautiful sunny morning where the captain proceeds to steer his boat to the exact location on the calm blue sea. From the Book of Common Prayer that I had hurriedly shoved into my luggage before leaving New York, I recite the prayer, "Earth to earth, ashes to ashes, dust to dust." Franklyn's sacred wishes had been observed and his spirit will loom large over his beloved village for eternity.

Our sojourn to the Motherland ends too quickly, and we soon return to Georgia. Juanita and I decide to go to a vacation spot called Helen that offers a nice refuge in the mountains where we go every year to escape the humdrum of everyday life and to mourn Franklyn's passing in the serenity of the wilderness. Soon upon our arrival, Nita complains she does not feel well. We treat her malaise as a reaction to the recent trip to St Vincent. The following day, we are out enjoying the surroundings, climbing up the hill to take a good view of the waterfall. Later that day, she complains again. I return to the hotel to hear Nita say, "I think I am pregnant." "Wait,"-unsure, doubting what I just heard—I said, "let me go buy a pregnancy test kit at the nearby pharmacy." I walk back while predicting . . . hoping . . . praying it was only a case of indigestion. However, after administering the test, the result comes back positive . . . she is pregnant with Vann. So, with the mystery put to rest, we continue our vacation and a few days later drive home knowing we were about to add another member to the Seales household.

On April 23, 1991 Vann Ellison Seales came into this world, nine months after scattering Franklyn's ashes at sea. The little boy must have been conceived on July 15, Franklyn's birthday. By the time Vann had reached his second birthday, Lennox became cognizant of Franklyn's prescient words spoken on that hospital bed, *"I want to give my mind to one of your children, Mike."* Chills go up and down his spine when he observes Vann's physicality, his emotional connection with them. Juanita, like Franklyn's mother Olive, had a hard time getting compliance from Vann. Like his uncle, he knows exactly what he wants to eat, clothes he wants to wear. At the age of nineteen, Vann is now a budding artist in his own right. Franklyn's will has been fulfilled, weird, bizarre as one might think. It is what it is.

Franklyn's body of work:

"Wiseguy" . . . . Paco Bazos (1 episode, 1988)

—Fascination for the Flame (1988) TV Episode . . . .
Paco Bazos

"Growing Pains" . . . . Dr. Jerry Marquez (1 episode,
1987)

—This Is Your Life" (1987) TV Episode . . . .Dr. Jerry
Marquez

"Amen" . . . . Lorenzo Hollingsworth (3 episodes,
1986-1987)

—Casting the First Stone" (1987) TV Episode . . . .
Lorenzo Hollingsworth

—Your Christmas Show of Shows (1986) TV Episode . . . .
Lorenzo Hollingsworth

—Pilot (1986) TV Episode . . . . Lorenzo Hollingsworth

"Silver Spoons" . . . . Dexter Stuffins (14 episodes,
1982-1983)

—Won't You Go Home, Bob Danish" (1983) TV
Episode . . . . Dexter Stuffins

—The Empire Strikes Out" (1983) TV Episode . . . .
Dexter Stuffins

—Three's a Crowd" (1983) TV Episode . . . . Dexter
Stuffins

—Junior Businessman" (1983) TV Episode . . . . Dexter
Stuffins

—The Toy Wonder (1983) TV Episode . . . . Dexter
Stuffins

The Taming of the Shrew (1983) (V) . . . . Petruchio

"Hill Street Blues" . . . . Crawford (3 episodes, 1982)

—No Body's Perfect (1982) TV Episode . . . . Crawford

—Phantom of the Hill (1982) TV Episode . . . . Crawford

—A Hair of the Dog (1982) TV Episode . . . . Crawford

Southern Comfort (1981) . . . . Pfc. Simms

Macbeth (1981) (V) . . . . Lennox

"Beulah Land" (1980) (mini) TV Series . . . . Roman

Star Trek: The Motion Picture (1979) . . . . Crew Member.

. . aka Star Trek: The Motion Picture—The Director's Edition (USA: DVD title)

The Onion Field (1979) . . . . Jimmy Lee 'Youngblood' Smith

The Trial of the Moke (1978) (TV) . . . . Lt. Henry O. Flipper

King Lear (1974) (TV) . . . . Servant to Cornwall

REFLECTIONS

"Our parents," Lennox muses, "were two people who without the benefit of advanced degrees and training, were experts in transmitting unconditional love to all of their children. Adding to this concept was Lessie. The most important thing that has happened to me and to us is the recognition of their unconditional love. We were touched by the energy and the power of Love. Things could have been worse. We could have been vested in fear but with the love we were blessed with, we were enabled to become successful people who were able to find their passions. Franklyn found his passion. He found what stirred his soul and put him in harmony with this universe.

"Ma taught us that it is possible to do difficult things, and do them well without losing one's self respect. Here is a woman that did menial jobs, denied herself while earning only $56.00 a week, yet found a way to open her home to newly arriving friends and family coming into this country. She never saw lack of material things as a hindrance to giving. She found the way to live and give to others less fortunate. She would often tell me, '*Son, if you could help somebody, then your living won't be in vain.*' At first it all sounded like crazy talk. However as the years went by, I truly believed that there was a method to her madness. She was an ordinary person doing extraordinary things. Ma expanded spiritually. She lived her beliefs and convictions. She would continue to give to strangers. One had to be careful giving her special gifts, for fear she would give it to the next visitor. After a while, it became the biggest joke among the children. We knew that Ma was always on a mission to give and to feed and open her home to family and friends in need. Overall, her secret is a spiritual principle. She served her family and others daily. She denied her self-interest. She loved, and that was what mattered. Giving was Ma's purpose in life."

The eleven month old baby girl named Natasha that Franklyn held in his arms upon his arrival in America in 1968 and counseled during her teenage years became a wife and mother of twins born in 2005.

"When I think of my uncle during the few stages of my life until he passed, my earliest memory is of the several paint tubes in his room, the paint easel with various dried paint colors on it and worn brushes. He would sit in front of his easel, focused, creating, expressing himself in beautiful ways. I appreciated his ability to focus and lay bare himself in the medium of a painting, in the form of his acting. He lost himself in that room in front of his piece of unfolding art as well as in his performance roles. I realized that he put forth the same focus and love toward me in so many ways.

"He was present from the beginning of my life to the end of his. His expression of love came in many forms—calls, letters, gifts, visits. I even knew that his questions about what I was feeling, thinking and doing were ways of demonstrating his love for me no matter how probing they seemed at the time. He wanted to make sure that I was happy, smiling and laughing which he always made sure you did with him. I have now surpassed his age at death and know that his lessons are with me. He left the example that there are no limits in life, only the ones you self impose. And most importantly, he left me with the ability to know that I should "live the life I love and love the life I live!" His ashes were taken to St. Vincent in late May 1990. My trip to St. Vincent for ten days was previously planned and was also purposeful in introducing my cousin Monique to the island. So, as God would have it, my trip was aligned with Uncle Franklyn's passing wish to have his ashes sprinkled in the Caribbean sea. It was nice for the family members that were there to be together during that time."

His sister Jennifer echoed similar sentiments:

"He loved the Christmas season. The highlights for him were caroling, nine mornings, and the Old Year's Nights fetes he attended at his friends' homes in Villa. Though at times he had many struggles and challenges with asthma and bronchitis, he remained a good scholar at the Boys Grammar school. Franklyn loved to laugh, hence he kept friends and family laughing too, with either his witty jokes or his comedic actions. His laughter at times was very boisterous and happy. Franklyn often advised those around him about hair, make-up and fashion. He taught us how to coordinate colors. I remember him teaching me to put on my make-up and styling my hair. At an early age, Franklyn was wise and talented beyond his years. We are all grateful for the many lessons we learned from him."

His childhood friend Antoinette would add:

"He wa a brother and the very best friend to me-I shared my secrets and dreams with him. He was unlike any of the boys or girls I knew. He was an entertainer as far back as I can remember-always ready to dance, sing, play the piano or try any instrument that was within his reach. All this came quite naturally to him . . . amazing isn't it? He instinctively knew that one day he would be famous, for he had plans and dreams, very confident at age fourteen that they would become as real as the sun rises each morning when he went to America. He would design fabulous gowns that he thought would be perfect for my then skinny little body . . . We once went to a dance at Crow's Nest-an established dance club which entertained the residents who would come from great distances to dance to the music; he was dressed as a girl. As expected he had the crowd laughing all night. He was great at telling stories that would have the family laughing while reenacting scenes. He was able to make me laugh even when I was sad. He knew how to have a good time and entertain while holding every one's attention. When he wasn't sketching outfits for me, he was composing a song or writing a story, trying a new dance. He was always working at something. Franklyn was a multi-talented guy and very comfortable in his own skin. We sure had a lot of laughs, and my mother loved him so very much."

Franklyn's nephew, Andy, shared much of the same remembrances expressed by the older siblings. Though they were seven years apart, he recalls an incidence that typifies his uncle's devilish sense of humor:

"Our aunt Ursie was spending the night at the house in one of the rooms. The toilet was located in the far end of the yard, so answering nature's call was not met by walking outside in the pitch darkness of the night, so a pot, commonly referred to as the "pozy" or colloquially the "pissy pot" was placed under the bed to relieve the bladder. One night, Franklyn tied a string to the handle of the pozy he anticipated aunt Ursie would use. We kids kept our eyes peeled and our ears against the partition until we heard movement in the adjoining room. She was readying herself to empty her bladder when at the appropriate time Franklyn began to slowly pull on the string sliding it away from auntie Ursie's orifice where the sun never shines. At that moment we heard her bellowing a screech repeating the words "oh my God, oh my Goodness, Inequity . . . Inequity" convinced an 'Obeah' spirit had entered the room. We almost died laughing and got an earful from her after discovering Franklyn's prank.

"On another occasion, Franklyn came home with a little male puppy he named "Zak" given to him by the

Russell family, owners of the movie theatre in town. All the kids in the neighborhood were drawn to Zak Franklyn took pleasure taking him to the beach with him. All the kids, I mean all of them, would follow Franklyn in tow to the water from whence Franklyn drew much of his energy. The kids took turns playing with Zak while others sat around Franklyn admiring the interaction. The ocean water held a very strong significance to him which is not easy to explain. He also held a fascination for books that he carried with him at all times, a habit that separated him from the rest of the kids. He drew much of his knowledge and inspirations from them. There was one particular hard cover book much larger than the average size book I saw him with that intrigued me since he had often times mentioned his passion for stamp collecting. After he left for America, I remained with my sister and brother in the care of Lessie. One day I stumbled on that very book he no doubt must have forgotten in his excitement. I opened it to discover an interesting thing; he had carved a hollow space in the book and filled it with his special collection of stamps that were carefully hidden from prying eyes."

The youngest of my sister Pat's three children was five-year-old Roger when his uncle left for America in 1968.

"My uncle and I were very close," he says, "he was kind and generous to me and to my brother Andy and sister Keithann to a fault. Even after he left for America, he always expressed his concerns for me. Before reaching my teens I had learned to hustle, to earn enough money to buy a pound of flour for Lessie to bake bread on

Saturdays. School for me was on the backburner; it was a matter of survival. When my brother and sister received their letters to join our mother in America, my aunt Jennifer joined me and Lessie to live with us. I was the last one left, but Uncle Franklyn would send me money. Thanks to him, I was able to open my first savings account at the bank in town. Me and Lessie survived on my uncle's generosity. I worked for yacht companies for years beginning at the age fourteen and fifteen to make ends meet. When I finally received my letter to join the family in New York, I met up with Franklyn who was very happy to get together. Even after my mother and her husband moved to Nashville, Franklyn came to visit and hang out with me. I can't tell you how much his passing hurt me. I have copies of his movie The Onion Field, copies of Silver Spoons on VHS I had transferred to DVD . . . When I want to have a good laugh, I pop them into the player and have a great time watching him. I'm so proud of my uncle . . ."

As his brother-in-law, I had much time to reflect about his short, happy and at times fractured life; what he accomplished and what he could have become but for the short time span he was assigned. Twenty years have gone by since we laid him to rest, yet a day does not come when I'm not reminded of his presence. I'm surrounded by his art, tapes of his movies, theatre reviews that chant of his enormous talents.

I recently sat down on my favorite reclining chair, a glass of Merlot on hand and lapsed into a state of euphoria while watching "The Trial of the Moke" transferred to DVD that Franklyn first performed with the Milwaukee Repertory Theater and adapted for television and broadcast on PBS in 1978. He had the lead role portraying Lt. Henry O. Flipper, the first black graduate of West Point. The supporting cast included very gifted actors, unknown then, but who became household names for the past thirty two years after its first telecast: Alfre Woodard, Samuel Jackson and the late Howard Rollins. I was again reminded of his outstanding talent and what he could have become in the company of celebrated Hollywood stars, Samuel Jackson and Alfre Woodard who have earned fame and fortune. I also looked at his portrayal of Paco Bazos in an episode of Wiseguy opposite another great actor, Kevin Spacey, a fellow Juilliard grad. His sister, Leslie, and I looked at his first feature movie in which he shares top billing with James Woods, The Onion Field that was first released in 1979. His dramatic performance arrests one's attention in every scene in which he appears. We watched several episodes of Silver Spoons that captured Franklyn's exceptional comedic timing as Dexter Stuffins. One episode dated 1986 features Franklyn's mentor from Juilliard, John Houseman, the man with exceptional instincts. Teacher and student reunited on the small screen. One sensed the pride in Mr. Houseman's appearance on that show that one of the pupils he recruited sixteen years earlier was making it in the public consciousness. We laughed so hard that the tears welled in our eyes seeing Franklyn memorialized on our TV screens for future generations that continue to expand the family tree like the majestic Savannah Live Oak Tree draped with Spanish Moss.

Twenty years already have passed since his ashes were flown into the wind and swallowed by the ocean on the shores of his beloved Calliaqua, much time to listen to my inner voice speaking to my brother-in-law:

Franklyn, I must confess that I hardly knew you. Our meeting in 1968 was our first, and the rest of your years passed in a blur. I read of your exploits. Conversations were shared among members of the family, always colored with much joy and pride, but for the most part, I failed to understand the essential Franklyn. I, nonetheless, want to thank you for the lessons you taught; most, I should add, subliminally. You taught me a very important aspect of the human spirit that many of us do not recognize in our journey through this life, that is encapsulated in the word "Intolerance," which to me, contrary to popular belief, is not essentially a "Vice" to be dismissed as wrong and by some, evil. You taught us, who were willing to think "outside the box," that intolerance can be raised to a level that can be viewed as a "Virtue." You never felt handicapped by the "lack" of anything or felt denied. Your spirit was much too rich to be mired in self-pity. You kept your blinders on and forged a path where there was none. You became the standard bearer for your peers, befuddled at first but years later arrived at the only sane conclusion: You were years ahead of them.

Your brother spoke candidly about your beginnings, what could have been construed as a sibling rivalry that lasted throughout your adult lives. He spoke of your single-mindedness that was a gift bestowed on you from the time you were able to recognize your environment, surrounded by family and friends. Unlike many who chose to live conventional lives, you acted intuitively, undeterred by the limitations others perceived as obstacles, but, which you regarded as challenges that molded the character of someone who could see beyond the visible. Unlike your peers who surrendered to the cards they were dealt with by life, you, by contrast had a vision of the impossible becoming possible. One can say, you were touched by an angel who took you under her wings and showed you the path.

You were blazing a trail that no one before you, on that paradise island, has ever walked on, triggering in their minds a litany of doubt, derision, mockery, and scorn, all traced to their limited visions. Undaunted, you showed them you knew the way and encouraged them to join you on that journey. Those who did, were better for it because they saw in you what they failed to see in themselves, but by emulating you, their lives were transformed.

It was heartbreaking to witness your passing. A life that brought so much joy to family, friends, and strangers alike. I found comfort though in the Word that reminds me: *"Where, O death, is thy victory? Where, O death, is thy sting?"* I still reminisce the days, the few years I observed you from afar. Believe me when I say that I found your steadfastness following your dreams a truly magnificent gift. As those closest to you say, "you were so very different from everyone. No one could fathom the forces at play in your life."

In retrospect, the lessons learned can inspire a new generation of artists spawned from your roots, Saint Vincent and the Grenadines. I know that your short and happy life has not been lived in vain when you came at the crossroads. You finally arrived at a place where all is forgiven; no more pain . . . no more need to validate your life goals. In a moment of clarity, I imagine you telling me:

"Jean, I was a man on a personal mission and led the life that was always part of me. I was also listening to my inner voice that convinced me that I was the captain of my ship. I was born too early . . . I know now that I had no hope of winning the battle against this disease that ravaged my body at the prime of my life . . . no one could help us then . . . I was destined for an early departure . . . many of my generation perished with me, Jean. My sole consolation is that I left you memories of my life's work on film and on canvas that I am sure you and the family cherish. Remember also, Jean, that in everyone of us lies a soul as pure as that of a child that loses its innocence in the pursuit of happiness. So was my destiny.

"Tell everyone that I'm doing fine now. You should see the audience I have here; in the millions and getting to perform 24/7 to standing ovations. There's no stopping Jean. You cannot understand how much I'm enjoying myself and how happy I am. My paintings, oh, you should see the colors I discovered that are indescribable and cannot be seen with the human eye. You should also know that Ma, Dad, grandmother, grandfather, Uncle Lawrence, Uncle Freddie, Uncle Arthur. Auntie Emmie, Auntie Athalie, Aunt Sis, Aunt Ursie, . . . we're all together. You should also know that Ma is no longer complaining. Ha!ha! It matters not what she lacked because she acquired what most in our mortal flesh do not have, it is everlasting Peace."

In the final analysis, whether by luck, destiny or Divine decree, whatever we make of ourselves in this mortal flesh will be measured by the imprints we leave in the sands of time. Franklyn's prints were notable and worth celebrating.

EPILOGUE

By virtue of my marriage to Leslie in 1965, I earned the title of "Senior Brother-in-Law" conferred upon me by her brother Michael Lennox Seales, first male born of the family of Francis and Olive Seales.

January 13, 1992, Francis Adolphus Seales departed this mortal coil in New York where he had resided since arriving in 1968. The children took the body home, St. Vincent and the Grenadines, the land of his ancestral tree.

Natasha, the one year old niece, Franklyn met on that hot summer July day 1968, married in 2001 and gave birth in 2005 to twins, Nadia and Benjamin IV. Franklyn, I know would have loved to play with them just as he did when he held his niece in his arms when he landed in America.

Lennox's toddler son Gabriel, Franklyn held in his arms in 1984, is now a twenty-seven-year-old married man with a two-year-old son of his own they named Oliver.

The three-week-old girl, Ashley, Franklyn met Christmas 1986 is a grown woman, college graduate in waiting for a proper suitor.

Franklyn's nanny, the venerable Lessie, died on March 5, 2003 at the age no one knows. Joy, Pat, Lennox, and Leslie immediately secured their passage from New York to their native land to pay tribute to this lady who, by all indications, they worshipped. I had no clue why her death would affect them all to such a degree. After all, she was a "nanny." Then, the story unfolded during my study of the history of my in-laws. It finally made sense to me why they would want to pay tribute to that most deserving woman who defined surrogate motherhood at its purest. It was only fitting they would return to their roots and reminisce about the good times with the woman they considered a second mother to them.

Tragedy revisited the Seales family when a phone call came from Savannah where mother Olive had relocated, telling us that her death came on November 23, 2003. She had fought many fights, and come to death door after two open-heart surgeries. She had finally succumbed after a long and courageous fight against the ravages of time.

BIBLIOGRAPHY

This Life—Sidney Poitier Ballantine books 1980

Caribbean Trailblazers—Baldwin King and Cheryl Phills King